The Bagel Bible

The Bagel Bible

For Bagel Lovers,
The Complete Guide to Great Noshing

by
Marilyn & Tom Bagel

The Globe Pequot Press

OLD SAYBROOK, CONNECTICUT

Library of Congress Cataloging-in-Publication Data

Bagel, Marilyn, 1946-
  The bagel bible : for bagel lovers, the complete guide to great noshing / by Marilyn and Tom Bagel.
    — 1st ed.
      p. cm.
  ISBN 1-56440-094-8
  1. Bagels. 2. Cookery (Bagels)   I. Bagel, Tom, 1944-   II. Title.
  TX770.B35B33 1992
  641.8'15—dc20   92-5790
                                               CIP

Book design by Nancy Freeborn
Illustrations by Lana Kleinschmidt
Author's cover photo by Andrea Fullen

Manufactured in the United States of America
First Edition/First Printing

Dedicated to bagel lovers everywhere,
especially Florrie, Alan and Amy, Evy and Aaron, Alice, and Jo-Anne and Marty.

Contents

CHAPTER 3 Handling and Storing Bagels 23

CHAPTER 4 Foolproof Bagel Baking in Your Kitchen 25

CHAPTER 5 Low-Fat, Low-Cal Feasts 33

CHAPTER 6 Breakfast Bagels 41

Contents

CHAPTER 7 Luncheon and Dinner Bagels 51

CHAPTER 8 Bagel Party Fare 77

CHAPTER 9 Children's Favorites 103

A Bagel Glossary 117

Bagel Buyer's Directory 121

Preface

You picked up this book because you love bagels or you know somebody who loves bagels. Perhaps your love affair with the "cement doughnut" began many years ago. Or maybe it was the result of a recent chance meeting at a carry-out when your eyes met a dazzling bronze-skinned bagel and you were hooked, like millions before you.

Whether you're an old fan or a relatively new admirer, *The Bagel Bible* by Marilyn and Tom Bagel is the definitive book on bagels by genuine Bagels. Tom was born and "bread" in Milwaukee. Marilyn became a Bagel by marriage.

So get ready to sink your teeth into dozens of creative bagel recipes for quick and easy meals any time of the day or night. And for those of you who want to try your hand at bagel baking, you'll also find recipes for making hot, crusty bagels in your own kitchen. Enjoy!

When made with kosher products, the recipes in this book are considered to be kosher.

Whatsa Bagel?

Bagels *should* be found in the dictionary under *fun,* but according to Webster (who probably liked his with a *shmear*) a bagel is "a hard roll shaped like a doughnut that is made of raised dough and cooked by simmering in water and then baked to give it a glazed brown exterior over a firm white interior." The bagel is the only bread product that is boiled before it is baked. That's what gives the bagel its unique texture and the crust its characteristic shine.

Legend has it that in 1683 in Vienna, Austria, a local Jewish baker wanted to thank the king of Poland for protecting his countrymen from Turkish invaders. He made a special hard roll in the shape of a riding stirrup—*Bügel* in German—commemorating the king's favorite pastime and giving the bagel its distinctive shape.

As bagels gained popularity in Poland, they were officially sanctioned as gifts for women in childbirth and mentioned in community registers. Mothers used them as nutritious teething rings that their infants could easily grasp—a practice still popular today.

Bagels eventually made their way to Russia, where they were called *bubliki* and were sold on strings. Like other ring-shaped objects, they were said to bring good luck and possess magical powers. It is even said that songs were sung about bagels!

1

An American Debut

When the Eastern European Jewish immigrants arrived in America at the turn of the century, they brought the bagel with them. The American bagel industry established formal roots in New York between 1910 and 1915 with the formation of Bagel Bakers Local #338. This exclusive group of 300 craftsmen with "bagels in their blood" limited its membership to sons of members. At the time, it was probably easier to get into medical school than to get an apprenticeship in one of the thirty-six union bagel shops in New York City and New Jersey.

Professional bagel baking required know-how and backbreaking labor. Bagel makers' sons apprenticed for months to learn the trade. Men were paid by the piece and usually worked in teams of four. Two made the bagels, one baked, and a "kettleman" was in charge of boiling the bagels. The men earned about 19 cents a box, and each box typically contained sixty-four bagels. It was not unusual for a team to make one hundred boxes a night.

With the rising of the yeast in countless bakeries, the popularity of the bagel rose far beyond the boundaries of ethnic neighborhoods. In the late 1950s and 1960s, bakers from New York and New Jersey began moving to other parts of the country. One such veteran who opened a bagel bakery in a suburb of Washington, D.C., in 1966, remembers his skeptical landlord nervously questioning, "Who's gonna spend 7 cents for one of *those* things?" Other bagel bakers who emigrated from Eastern Europe settled in Canada, giving cities like Toronto and Montreal their reputation for superb bagels.

Prepackaged bagels first became available in grocery stores in the 1950s. With the introduction of frozen bagels in the 1960s, consumers had access to bagels even if they didn't live near a bagel bakery.

Bagel-making machines, a boon to commercial bakers, were also introduced in the early 1960s. Inventor Dan Thompson says, "I was born to invent a bagel machine. My father was thinking about a bagel-making machine when I was conceived." That may not be far from the truth, because Dan's father had a wholesale bakery in Winnipeg, Canada, and was already working on a bagel-making machine back in 1926. But it was far too complicated, too slow, and too costly to manufacture and it wasn't commercially feasible.

There were as many as fifty unsuccessful attempts to produce a bagel-making machine

Hot news for good nutrition

in the early twentieth century. The Thompson Bagel Machine Corporation developed the first viable model, despite "doubting Thompsons" who insisted that no machine would ever replace the human hand. Most of the early machines were leased by bakers who paid by the dozen on a running timemeter. Now most are purchased. One model can form 200 dozen bagels an hour, another as many as 400 dozen an hour.

You've Come a Long Way, Bagel

Bagels are not just for breakfast anymore; in recent years, consumer demand for bagels has absolutely exploded in this country, with sales approaching $1 billion a year in the United States alone. Today considered no more "ethnic" than pizza or tacos, bagels are a mainstay on tables in households of every race, creed, color, and religion.

Major corporations have entered the bagel market in a big way, not just with bagels but also with a host of bagel products, from bagel chips to bagel "dogs." Fast-food chains have bagels on the menu. You can find bagels at your local supermarket—at the bakery counter, in the bread section, at the deli counter, in special self-serve bins, and in the freezer section—and at bagel bakeries, convenience stores, department stores, even doughnut shops. Some bagel bakeries are open twenty-four hours a day, to satisfy the needs of true bagelholics. It's a far cry from pushcart sales on cobblestone streets at the turn of the century.

Commercial bagel bakers are responding to this bagel love affair not only by extending their product lines but by refining mass production techniques. Some companies are steaming instead of boiling the bagels prior to baking. In this process, racks of bagels are rolled into upright steam-injected rack ovens. This speeds production and results in a softer bagel that lends itself more readily to sandwich making: The fillings won't squeeze out when you bite into the sandwich. However, diehards argue that it's not a bagel unless the filling "squishes" out when you bite into it!

The Low-fat, No-cholesterol Wonder

Bagels are a dream come true if you're watching your weight, your cholesterol, or your fat intake. You'll find bagels on the recommended list of every major diet plan. They have no

cholesterol and very little fat. They are highly satisfying, and their chewiness makes them much more emotionally gratifying than a slice of bread. Take a fresh bagel along for a filling low-fat snack, particularly if you plan to be someplace—such as on an airplane—where your food choices will be limited.

Bagels vary in size from baker to baker and manufacturer to manufacturer. They can range from 1-ounce bagelettes (miniature bagels) to mega-bagels that tip the scales at over 5 ounces. On the average, you can figure on the following nutritional content for a 2.5-ounce plain bagel:

37	grams carbohydrate
8	grams protein
1	gram fat
0	milligrams cholesterol
450	milligrams sodium
190	calories

Bagels Are Even Good for Your Love Life

The "teddy bear of foods," bagels bring out the best in everyone. Even the most unemotional people you know will wax poetic when you ask them what their favorite bagel flavor is!

Share a bagel and you have a friend for life. Business goes better with bagels. Arguments are more civilized over bagels and coffee. Making up is more loving with bagels and champagne. And if you want to make a lasting impression, forget the dozen roses. Just bring a dozen hot bagels and some cream cheese. You'll make a big hit and save a lot of money too.

Bagel Styles of
the Rich and Famous

W hat food other than a bagel could make such a distinguished assemblage of glitterati react with wild abandon . . . practically weep with joy . . . in other words, go bonkers over bagels? Here's what the "Who's Who" have to say about *their* bagels.

Jane Alexander

This highly acclaimed stage, television, and film actress is known for her memorable portrayals, but Jane's love of bagels is no act.

> *"I eat five or six bagels a week. I had my first bagel in 1960, and my favorite kind is plain—with the hole! My favorite way of eating them is with my teeth. I've tried all kinds of bagels, but I like plain ones the best. The strangest way I've ever eaten bagels is with refried beans. Why do I like bagels? They're chewy and exercise my jawline."*

Meredith Baxter

This versatile, talented actress enjoys her roles in front of the camera. But her favorite "roll" behind the scenes is a bagel!

> *"I love garlic and onion bagels. I first started eating bagels about thirty years ago and find their shape wonderfully appealing. I have three a week when I'm working, but none when I'm not. My favorite way of eating them is toasted very crisp—black on the edges—with scads of butter. For me, the strangest thing I've ever had on a bagel is cream cheese. I guess the reason I haven't experimented more with bagels is that I'm inhibited!"*

David Brenner

A well-known comedian who always performs to packed houses, Brenner enjoys relaxing with well-packed bagels.

> *"I love eating my bagels 1) with my hands; 2) with thickly piled cream cheese and smooth peanut butter; 3) with cream cheese and tuna; 4) with cream cheese and crisp bacon. I especially love untoasted plain or pumpernickel bagels. I've been eating them since I was two months and three days old. On a good week I eat between 2,500 and 3,200."*

Jane Brody

This noted cookbook author and *New York Times* "Personal Health" columnist is an expert on nutritious foods. That's why bagels are a mainstay in her bread basket practically every day.

> *"I first started eating bagels somewhere between the ages of six months and a year old. My favorite kind is sesame seed. I eat about five to seven bagels a week. I prefer them au naturel. I simply break off chunks and eat them plain. The strangest combination I've ever put on a bagel is caviar and sour cream—raising the bagel to new heights! I haven't done more experimenting because I like them just the way they come out of the oven. They're so chewy and satisfying."*

Dr. Joyce Brothers

Dr. Joyce Brothers is a noted psychologist, radio and television personality, columnist, and author, whom millions of people rely on as a source of wisdom, common sense, and practical advice. According to Dr. Brothers, bagels play a significant "roll" in childhood.

> *"I first started eating bagels as an infant. My favorite kind of bagel is plain, and I eat a couple every week with cream cheese. Bagels are the best teething rings ever devised. They will keep a small child or infant, who's old enough to sit up and grasp an object, entertained and happy longer than anything else."*

Jerry Buss

Jerry Buss, real estate company executive and owner of the Los Angeles Lakers basketball team, says that although it's baskets that count on the court, off the court it's a basket of bagels.

> *"I first started eating bagels ten years ago. My favorite are raisin bagels, especially at breakfast time when they're toasted, spread with butter or cream cheese, and served with bacon and eggs. They taste so good that I have to limit myself."*

Dick Clark

Creator, producer, and host of many of the country's most widely viewed television series and specials, and a driving force in American music, Clark gives bagels a "100"—they have a great beat and are fun to dance to.

> *"I first started eating bagels in the 1930s. My favorite kind is plain. I have one or two a week. I like them toasted with cream cheese. The strangest combination I've ever had on a bagel is peanut butter and pickles. I would experiment more, but I still bear a scar on the third finger of my left hand from a knife I used during an unsuccessful bagel experiment!!!"*

William Conrad

This highly accomplished stage and television actor, producer, director, and narrator, is also an acknowledged chili gourmet who thinks bagels are *really* hot stuff.

"I first started eating bagels at the tender age of three. My favorite kinds are salt, poppy seed, pumpernickel, raisin, rye—any water bagel, no egg bagels. I try to hold down the quantity to a baker's dozen a week. Bagels are sooo good! My favorite way of eating bagels is to toast them, then spread them with cream cheese and chives and fresh chopped jalapeño peppers. The strangest thing I've ever eaten on a bagel is chili con carne with rattlesnake meat. When it comes to bagels, I'm the best bagel experimenter on my block!"

Norm Crosby

This popular entertainer and wordsmith extraordinaire has a unique way of expressing himself. But ask Norm for a monologue on bagels, and he gives it to you straight.

"I started eating bagels when I was very young. I also played with them as a baby. They're difficult to chew with no teeth. I eat at least a half-dozen a week, especially pumpernickel. I like them toasted with cream cheese or open-face with tuna fish and a slice of onion. Actually, I've tried everything on bagels—hot dogs, caviar (not together!), mustard—and I often make a pickle sandwich using bagels. I like bagels because they're quick to prepare, tasty, and good for you. If these sensible reasons aren't enough, I like 'em 'cause they're bagels and maybe because I don't like anything square!"

Fred de Cordova

De Cordova, the well-known producer-director of NBC's "The Tonight Show," thinks bagels have star quality. For Fred it's "Lights! Cameras! Bagels!"

"Why do I like bagels? Because bagels like me. I entered puberty with a bagel. That's when I first started eating them. Now my week wouldn't be complete without at least one.

I would have experimented more with bagels if it hadn't been for parental warnings. Bagels can be habit-forming!"

Phyllis Diller

A well-known comedienne and popular entertainer, Phyllis Diller has them rolling in the aisles with her repartee, and her observations about bagels are no exception.

"Even the thought of bagels is an inspiration to me. I bet you didn't know that when Ronald Reagan ran for president, he was so gung ho to get all the ethnic votes, he went into a deli and ordered a bagel. The waiter said, 'How would you like that?' Ronnie said, 'On rye.' Incidentally, my advice is never eat a day-old bagel. There is a day-old bagel someplace in this world with teeth in it—mine! By the way, did you hear about the new Bagel Diet? You just eat the holes."

Olympia Dukakis

This accomplished actress always delivers memorable performances in roles she can really sink her teeth into. But the starring "roll" she tackles with gusto is a bagel.

"I've been eating bagels for over thirty years. I like sesame best of all. I eat about three bagels a week. I guest you could say I'm a traditionalist at heart, because my favorite way of eating bagels is still with cream cheese and lox. However, I have gone so far as to have a bagel with banana, mayonnaise, and peanut butter on it. I love bagels because they're soft inside and have such a wonderful taste.

Whoopi Goldberg

Whoopi Goldberg, gifted Academy Award–winning actress and comedienne, has nourished her natural acting talents with years of bagel eating.

"I first started eating bagels as a kid in New York. I really like salted bagels the best. I

have about four or five a week, usually toasted with butter. Bagels are great because they're chewy and satisfying! Who needs a pretzel when you have a bagel?"

Mark Goodson

The consummate innovative producer, Goodson has created many of television's most memorable, successful, and classic game shows, past and present, including "I've Got a Secret," "Beat the Clock," "The Price Is Right," and "Family Feud." Mark has absolutely no difficulty answering questions about bagels!

"I ate my first bagel in Sacramento—that sounds like the title of a song—when I was about ten. My favorite kind of bagel is good old-fashioned plain—with cream cheese (natch!) and smoked fish (natch!). No matter how many I eat, it's never enough. The strangest thing I've ever eaten on a bagel is caviar once, but I really haven't experimented because, bagel-wise, I'm a conservative. I like bagels because I love crusty things, and the taste of a bagel is redolent of my youth."

Heloise

This trusted "Dean of Household Hints" shares the suggestions of millions of fans in her widely read column, which appears in newspapers from coast to coast. Heloise will tell you that you should always have some bagels on hand, because no household is complete without them.

"Why do I like bagels? What's not to like!? I first started eating bagels in Washington, D.C., as a child. My favorite is whole wheat and, though I eat none when I'm in Texas, I eat as many as I can when I'm in New York. I like bagels with cream cheese, onion, and tomatoes, or peanut butter and cream cheese. Actually, nothing is too strange to put on a bagel."

"As you can see, Dahling, I only do starring rolls. . . ."

Bob Hope

The premier Global Showman has faced millions of adoring fans the world over with ease. But he finds facing a bagel his greatest challenge.

> *"I remember the first time I ate a bagel. It was also the first time I broke a tooth. My favorite kind is a soft one, if it can be found. How many do I eat? Maybe one a year. My favorite way of eating them is with a doctor on hand. The strangest thing I've ever eaten on a bagel is vegetable soup. I haven't experimented more with bagels, because I prefer to eat doughnuts before they're soaked in cement. Why do I like bagels? . . . Why do I like the I.R.S.?"*

Marty Ingels

Marty Ingels, a man of many talents—actor, comic, writer, and Hollywood Super Agent—always knows what's "in" and what's "out" . . . and, of course, the super-scoop on bagels. To quote the Brooklyn Boychik:

> *"Actually, it wasn't till I was fourteen that I realized they were edible. They were always piled up and stuck together in the freezer. My mother talked about keeping 'onions' in them . . . and 'seeds' . . . even 'water.' And we could only buy them on certain days and only from a very fat man named Itzhak who dribbled when he spoke. Why would anyone want to eat one of those? (Once one of them fell out of the fridge onto my father's foot and broke two of his toes. Most kids I knew were scared of them.)*
>
> *They were much easier to digest when I was a kid. 'Got a very sensitive stomach these days, so I take them intravenously. And people really differ on their health effect. My doctor once told me that he put absolutely no limit on the number of bagels he himself ate. But last week his widow left a message on my service to call her about that. And people like them with different things—with butter, with cheese, with lox, even with meat. I like mine with an ambulance. Somebody once asked me what was the strangest combina-*

14

tion I ever put on a bagel. I once put a twenty-eight-year-old hooker named Beulah on one and turned the lights out. (She now lives on a kibbutz just south of Haifa, and they say she's doing very well.) For a while, I tried "experimenting" with bagels, but I lost the grant.

Why do I like bagels?—No jokes? Because they bring me back to a sweeter, simpler time when good was good and bad was bad and right was right and wrong was wrong and we may not've known a hell of a lot, but we knew which was which and when. Today I'm not sure of anyone—or anything—except my bagel.

Shirley Jones Ingels

Shirley Jones, America's sweetheart, whose Oscar-winning career has included the movies *Oklahoma!, Carousel, The Music Man,* and *Elmer Gantry,* and the long-running television series "The Partridge Family," confides that she deserves an Oscar for living with husband Marty . . . and eating bagels.

"I first started eating bagels in 1977. Marty wrote it into our prenuptial agreement after he saw me order corned beef with mayonnaise. How many bagels do I eat a week? That depends on how often my in-laws visit (and how much mayonnaise I have in the house). My favorite way of eating bagels is with communion wafers. But the most gratifying combination I've ever put on a bagel is Bromo and Maalox. I haven't experimented with bagels because Marty said something about how eating them with anyone other than your husband constitutes some sort of Hebrew adultery. Why do I like bagels? I've lived long enough."

Larry King

America's favorite television and radio talk-show host, has been a bagel eater since birth. He really knows what he likes. Besides, bagels don't talk back!

"Bagels have a taste all their own. They are perfectly named: They fill, they bring pleasure—they are bagels! I eat about five or six a week. I especially like salt bagels. My favorite way of eating them is with lox and cream cheese. All others are frauds."

15

Ed McMahon

Host of the syndicated program "Star Search," Ed McMahon was for many years television's most celebrated sidekick, on "The Tonight Show." What else would you expect Ed to say about his favorite bagel but *"Heeere's onion!"*

> *"Onion bagels are number one with me. I eat three or four a week. I first started eating bagels while in the service during World War II. My favorite way of eating them is toasted with peanut butter or cream cheese and lox. I haven't tried other combinations because of my inherent shyness. Why do I like bagels? Because they're delicious! What better reason?"*

Marvin Mitchelson

This famed palimony and divorce attorney to the stars says the splits he *really* likes to work on are two bagel halves.

> *"I've been eating bagels for over forty years. My favorite kind is pumpernickel. I usually eat from two to five a week and love them hollowed out, with lox, onion, and whitefish—no cream cheese. The strangest combination I've ever had on a bagel is banana and cottage cheese. Why do I like bagels? The indefinable feeling of being Jewish."*

John Moschitta, Jr.

John Moschitta is the uniquely talented television personality who began fast-talking his way into millions of American living rooms with his memorable commercials for Federal Express. The faster John speaks, the more time he has to eat bagels nice and slow!

> *"You never forget your first bagel. I had mine on Tuesday, July 14, 1957, at 10:07 a.m. My favorite kind is poppy seed. I have two a week. The strangest combination I've ever had on a bagel is pineapple with spaghetti sauce. But my all-time favorite way of eating bagels is with chopped liver, turkey, coleslaw, Muenster cheese, lettuce, and tomato. I call it the 'mighty mouthful!' Bagels taste great any time and any way, plus you can play ring-toss with them."*

Paloma Picasso-Lopez

This world-class designer and savvy businesswoman heads a signature line that includes jewelry, scarves, handbags, perfume, cosmetics, china, crystal, and silver with great panache. She credits bagels as her inspiration.

"Since I am French, I did not grow up on bagels, but I had my first one in 1968. My favorite kind is plain. It's difficult to say how many I eat a week, because I don't spend that much time in America. Besides, I am always on a diet! I particularly enjoy eating bagels with smoked Scottish salmon. The strangest combination I've ever had on a bagel is mashed potatoes on a bed of lettuce with olive-oil vinaigrette. I would be even more inventive if I had more free time and did less dieting. I'm afraid of all the good things I can create. Why do I like bagels? Because of the taste and the look. You might notice there is a similarity—a definite connection—between my designs and bagels."

Ahmad Rashad

Ahmad Rashad, popular member of the NBC Sports broadcast team, was also a star football player for the Minnesota Vikings. But he fills *his* super bowl with bagels.

"I'm a basic, uncomplicated kind of guy. As a snack, I like my bagels not toasted with grape jelly and cream cheese. As a real meal, I like them toasted with cream cheese and grape jelly."

Phyllis Richman

Executive food editor and restaurant critic for *The Washington Post,* Phyllis Richman is a bagel purist. She started eating bagels as soon as she had teeth, and she's been giving bagels critical acclaim ever since.

"My favorite kind of bagel is a good one. But I won't tell you how many I eat a week. That's top secret! Now as to how I like eating them . . . is there any other way than with

nova and cream cheese? You don't mess around with perfection! Why do I like bagels?"
That's like asking why I like breathing!"

Geraldo Rivera

Geraldo Rivera, controversial and widely viewed talk-show host, is well known for his penetrating style and investigative reporting. Geraldo investigated his first bagel more than twenty years ago and has been enthusiastically digging into the subject ever since.

"I started eating bagels around 1965 when I moved to New York after college. My favorite kind is poppy seed. I eat two or three a week, either toasted or untoasted, with cream cheese and olives—olives in between the bagel and the cream cheese. The strangest thing I've ever eaten on a bagel is not so strange at all—raisins. I'm very conservative about my culinary adventures, so I haven't experimented more. Why do I like bagels? They are tastier, funnier, and more creative than plain bread. And they taste great with cream cheese and olives!"

Joan Rivers

This popular talk-show host and comedienne is never at a loss for words, especially about bagels.

"I first started eating bagels when I was twenty minutes old. That's when I had a bagel and a Hershey bar! My favorite bagels are the ones with the hole in the center. I love all varieties. How many do I eat a week? I stop counting after Tuesday. My favorite way of eating a bagel is as a sandwich, filled with a pepperoni pizza. The strangest thing I've ever eaten on a bagel is a banana split. Why do I like bagels? They seem to like me. They go right to my thighs and just won't leave."

Phil Rizzuto

Phil Rizzuto, one of the most popular Yankees of all time, is also the team's legendary broadcaster. When Phil rounds the plate, there's always a bagel on it. Holy cow!

"I eat at least a half-dozen bagels a week. I've been eating bagels ever since 1937. My favorite kinds are salt and plain, with cream cheese, lox, and chive cheese. The strangest combination I've ever had on a bagel is jelly, bananas, and cream cheese. Why do I like bagels? They're the best, especially in the morning and late evening."

Willard Scott

Willard Scott, NBC "Today Show" personality and television host of "The New Original Amateur Hour," is America's favorite weatherman. According to Willard, the national radar weather map picks up bagels from coast to coast.

"Today's forecast is a sesame-seed bagel, my favorite kind! Take it from ol' Willard, bagels are the greatest. Especially sesame bagels piled high with cream cheese. I eat them every chance I get. Now if I could only figure out how to grow bagels on my farm!"

Doc Severinsen

Famed concert artist and for years the music director of "The Tonight Show" band on NBC-TV, Doc admits to putting down his trumpet for a bagel.

"My favorite bagel arrangement is ham on an egg bagel. I've found that bagels are not only high in food value, they're also useful for construction purposes."

Artie Shaw

This legendary clarinet virtuoso, bandleader, and arranger says that bagels have been music to his ears for years!

> *"I first started eating bagels sometime before or during the first Crusade. I love onion bagels, sesame bagels, plain bagels—any kind at all, just so it's a bagel. How many do I eat? About six or eight a week. I usually have them toasted with butter. Why, is there any other way? I'm your basic straight-ahead bagel type—nothing strange, nothing kinky. Asking me why I like bagels is like asking why I like breathing air or drinking water. All bagels are good and good for you, too. So what's not to like?"*

Liz Smith

The widely read syndicated show-biz columnist of *Newsday* knows bagels make good press, especially with cream cheese.

> *"I had never even seen a bagel until 1949 when I came to New York and had my first one. I've tried peanut butter on bagels but haven't experimented more because I'm too gentile and cowardly. I love sesame bagels and would eat more of them, but I have to ration myself! My favorite way to eat a bagel is toasted with lots of butter and cream cheese. Bagels are delicious and a challenge to eat."*

Abigail Van Buren

Abigail Van Buren, whose syndicated "Dear Abby" advice column is read and followed by millions of devoted readers, advises you to eat at least one bagel every day.

> *"I've been eating bagels ever since I had teeth. My favorite kind is an egg bagel. I go on sporadic bagel binges and eat bagels every day for a week. Then I knock off for a while.*

My favorite way of eating a bagel is to slice it lengthwise, toast it, and load on the butter and cream cheese. I've also enjoyed caviar on bagels—a very expensive frivolity indeed, but worth it! I haven't experimented more because I'm happy with my present mode of eating bagels. I love them because they're delicious. Why else?"

Diane Von Furstenberg

This well-known designer, who heads one of the country's most successful dressmaking companies, is responsible for putting the "little print wrap dress" in the closet of every fashion-conscious woman in America. But what she enjoys wrapping her hands around is a bagel.

"I first started eating bagels when I was a child. I like bagels because they remind me of my father, because they are cozy like little pillows."

Duke Zeibert

Host to many of the most powerful people in the nation's capital, restaurateur Duke Zeibert is also a "roll-model" for bagel lovers everywhere.

"I eat bagels every day of the week, especially pumpernickel with cream cheese and mustard. I've been eating bagels for so many years now, I can't recall. Bagels give me wisdom and strength. Let's face it. How else could I settle petty differences between the chef, pastry chef, roll baker, and head waiter—and try to keep them all?"

Lox, stocked, and bageled

3

Handling
and Storing Bagels

You can eat bagels any way you like—toasted, heated, or fresh from the bag. Everybody quickly develops a personal style. Some people only eat bagels toasted; others think it's heresy to toast them. Some cut them in half; others only eat them whole. And that's just for starters—it doesn't include all the individual flavor preferences!

Any way you slice them, bagels are a deliciously versatile experience. They sit up tall, proud, and golden-brown, waiting to be sliced, spread, topped, or scooped out and filled.

If you buy your bagels at a bakery where they're continuously baked, you'll often get them hot from the oven. If you're buying more than you plan to eat the same day, simply freeze the rest. If they're still hot, let them cool first before transferring them to plastic bags for freezing. This prevents them from getting soggy.

Cut your bagels in half before freezing them so you'll have the option of having the equivalent of a whole or half bagel whenever the mood strikes. You can toast your bagels frozen, or if you like them heated rather than toasted, put them in the oven or toaster oven for about five minutes at 400°.

You can freshen days-old bagels by putting them in a covered pot with a few drops of water and placing the pot in a preheated 350° oven for ten minutes or so. But frankly, it makes much more sense to freeze bagels instead of letting them sit around . . . unless you want to use them for paperweights, doorstops, or hockey pucks, or give them to the dog!

Toaster manufacturers have become quite accommodating to bagel lovers. They've come out with toaster models with larger-than-standard-size openings, so you might want to be on the lookout for one of these. If you have a toaster oven, all the better. It makes toasting or heating a snap no matter how big your bagels are.

Be aware that heating bagels in the microwave oven changes their consistency, making them somewhat rubbery. Use a microwave as a last resort, heating bagels for just a few seconds at a time. You *can* use the microwave to *defrost* frozen bagels successfully (fifty seconds on the DEFROST setting). You can also use your microwave to restore stale bagels from the frozen state (approximately seventy seconds on the DEFROST setting).

Please note that many of the recipes in this book call for the use of a foil-covered cookie sheet. We find that this makes for quick and easy cleanup. Once you remove the aluminum foil, your cookie sheet is instantly clean.

4

Foolproof Bagel Baking in Your Kitchen

If you've been unsuccessful at baking bagels in the past, your troubles are over: Here are recipes for homemade bagels you can brag about. If you've never tried to bake bagels before, get ready to be a first-time pro. Bagel making is fun, and it's a wonderful way to spend a couple of hours on a rainy day . . . or any time. Try your hand at it—you'll be deliciously rewarded.

Professional bagel baking is a tricky process. Making good bagels depends on many factors, each of which can significantly affect the outcome: the proper quality of high-gluten flour (commercial bakers use varieties not available in supermarkets); the water quality (hence the need for bakeries' water-purification systems in some areas); the right quantity of yeast; the right amount of salt (too much affects the dough's ability to rise); the expertise of the dough maker; the mixing; the boiling method; and so on. Weather conditions are also a factor. As one bagel baker puts it, "Bagel dough is like a human being—it senses temperature." When the weather is warm, bakers use less yeast. In humid or dry conditions, they make other adjustments.

In a professional bagel bakery, after the bagels are formed and have risen, they are placed in a refrigeration unit known as a *retarder*, which retards the rising process and also affects the formation of the crust. The retarder has a lower humidity than a standard refrigerator. Kettling—boiling the bagels—helps form the bagel "skin" and gives bagels their special shine.

Most professionals favor dry yeast over cake yeast, because it's easier to store. They have flour preferences as well. In fact, bagel bakers are so savvy, they can tell which brand of flour their competitors use and even when and if they switch brands.

In some bagel bakeries, the first stage of bagel baking takes place on burlap-covered redwood boards. The burlap boards are wet down with water; the bagels are then placed on the boards and put in the oven. Among bagel bakers, the expression "flipping the boards" describes the step of turning the bagels over from burlap boards onto the oven hearth.

Perhaps your neighborhood bagel bakers can take a moment when they're not too busy (although that's rare) and give you a behind-the-scenes peek.

Lucky for bagel lovers everywhere, we've streamlined the bagel-making process for easy home baking. Even if you're a beginner, these recipes will guide you step-by-step to delicious homemade bagels.

Basic No-Fail Bagels

This recipe is based on techniques used by professional bagel bakers. It makes sixteen delicious 3½-ounce bagels. You can bake them plain or, by adding different toppings just before baking, create an assortment of your favorites—for example, four sesame seed, four poppy seed, four garlic, and four onion bagels.

Two .6-ounce cakes fresh yeast or two ¼-ounce packets active dry yeast
2 teaspoons sugar (only if using dry yeast)
2½ teaspoons salt

6⅛ cups high-gluten bread flour
½ cup yellow cornmeal
Sesame seeds, poppy seeds, dehydrated onion flakes, dehydrated or fresh
minced garlic

1. *If you use cake yeast:* Be sure to note the expiration date printed on the package. If you have any doubt as to its freshness, crumble it; cake yeast is good if it crumbles readily. Dissolve the yeast completely in 2½ cups *cool water* in a large mixing bowl. Let stand for 5 minutes. Proceed to Step 2. *If you use dry yeast:* Place the yeast in a glass with ½ cup *warm water* (the water should feel warm to your fingertips). Stir in the 2 teaspoons of sugar. Mix until the yeast is dissolved completely and set aside in a draft-free place for 5 minutes. The mixture should bubble up, producing a foamy layer on top. (If it doesn't bubble up, you probably used water that was too hot and killed the yeast, in which case you'll have to discard it and start again. If you have any doubts about the temperature, it's better to use water that's too cool.) Pour the mixture into a large mixing bowl and add 2 cups *lukewarm* water.

2. Stir in the salt. Add 5½ cups flour, a cup at a time, mixing with a wooden spoon to blend after each addition. Dough will be sticky.

3. Spread ¼ cup flour on a tabletop or other kneading surface. Place the dough on the flour. (You may have some dry flour remaining in the mixing bowl. Shake that onto the dough as well.) Place an additional 1/4 cup of flour on top of the dough.

4. Begin kneading slowly until the flour comes together with the rest of the dough. Then knead vigorously for 15 minutes. It may be necessary to add a bit more flour if the mixture is sticky. (That's what the extra ⅛ cup is for.) *Note:* Sometimes—on a humid day, for instance—your dough may still be sticky and difficult to knead even *after* you add the ⅛ cup flour. At these times, simply dip your hands in the flour, shake off the excess, and continue kneading. You can do this as often as necessary. Just be sure not to add additional flour to the dough. Your floured hands will be sufficient.

5. Using a sharp knife dipped in flour, cut the dough into sixteen equal sections.

27

Doctor of Hole-istic Medicine

6. Take a section of dough and roll it in your palms to make a ball. Poke your thumbs through the center and work around to make a hole a bit larger than the size of a quarter. Repeat with the remaining sections.

7. Spread ¼ cup cornmeal on each of two trays or wooden cutting boards and place eight formed bagels on each, about 1 inch apart. Cover with a clean dish towel and place in a warm, draft-free spot for 45 minutes to rise. (An *unheated* oven is a perfect place.)

8. Remove towel and place boards or trays of bagels in refrigerator for 1 hour.

9. Meanwhile, preheat the oven to 400°. In a large pot, bring 3 quarts of water to a boil.

10. Prepare two cookie sheets by spreading them with some additional cornmeal.

11. After you've refrigerated the bagels for an hour, remove them and place them, four at a time, in the boiling water. This stage is called *kettling*. The perfect bagel, when kettled, should sink to the bottom of the pot of boiling water and rise immediately. Boil for about 4 minutes, turning the bagels over about every 30 seconds or so with a slotted spoon. If your bagels don't sink to the bottom when you first put them in the pot, don't worry. However, if they sink to the bottom and lie there, wait until they rise to the top (and they will) before timing your 4 minutes.

12. After kettling, remove the bagels with a slotted spoon and place them on top of a clean towel for a few seconds to drain off excess water. Then place the bagels on the cookie sheets (eight on each). Liberally sprinkle them with your favorite toppings. (Some people like to brush beaten egg on top before sprinkling toppings on. This makes a crustier bagel, which we do not recommend.)

13. Bake for 35 minutes, or until golden. Watch the bagels carefully toward the end of the baking time because every oven is different. After taking them out of the oven, remove the bagels from the cookie sheets and let them cool on a wire rack for 10 minutes—which will take all the willpower you have!

Makes 16 bagels

Whole-Wheat Bagels

2 packages active dry yeast
3 tablespoons honey
1 tablespoon salt
2 cups whole-wheat flour
2¾ cups high-gluten bread flour
1 tablespoon sugar
¼ cup yellow cornmeal

1. Mix the yeast and 2 cups of warm water (about 110°) in a large bowl, and let stand for 5 minutes. Stir in the honey and salt.

2. In a smaller bowl, mix the whole-wheat flour with 1¼ cups of the bread flour. Using an electric mixer, add the flour mixture to the yeast mixture a bit at a time. When all of the flour has been incorporated, beat for about 4 minutes.

3. Add the remaining 1½ cups of bread flour and beat by hand. Dough will be stiff.

4. Turn the dough out on a liberally floured surface (such as a countertop or kitchen table), and knead for 15 minutes, or until smooth. If the dough is still sticky, add more bread flour a bit at a time and knead until it is not.

5. Place the dough in a bowl and cover with a clean dish towel. Place in a warm, draft-free spot for about 45 minutes to rise (an *unheated* oven is perfect). The dough will double in size.

6. Knead the dough gently for 1 minute and cut it into twelve pieces.

7. Take a section of dough and roll it in your palms to make a ball. Poke your thumbs through the center and work around to make a hole a bit larger than the size of a quarter. Repeat with the remaining sections.

8. Place the bagels on a lightly floured wooden cutting board, cover with a dish towel, and place in a warm, draft-free spot for 20 minutes.

9. Meanwhile, preheat the oven to 400°. Bring 3 quarts of water to a boil; add 1 teaspoon of sugar.

10. Follow the kettling and baking instructions on page 29 (steps 10 through 13).

Makes 12 bagels

Cinnamon-Raisin Bagels

These are so good, your family will swear you made a quick trip to the bagel store when they weren't looking.

2 packages active dry yeast
3 tablespoons honey
1 tablespoon salt
2¾ cups high-gluten bread flour
1½ cups golden raisins
1 tablespoon ground cinnamon
2 tablespoons sugar
2 cups whole-wheat flour
¼ cup yellow cornmeal

1. Mix the yeast and 2 cups of warm water (about 110°) in a large bowl, and let stand for 5 minutes. Stir in the honey and salt.

2. In a smaller bowl, mix the whole-wheat flour, 1¼ cups of the bread flour, cinnamon, and sugar. Using an electric mixer, add the flour mixture to the yeast mixture a bit at a time. When all of the flour has been incorporated, beat for about 4 minutes.

3. Add the remaining 1½ cups of bread flour and beat by hand. Dough will be stiff.

4. Turn the dough out on a liberally floured surface (such as a countertop or kitchen table),

31

and knead for 15 minutes, or until smooth. If the dough is still sticky, add more bread flour a bit at a time and knead until it is not.

5. Place the dough in a bowl and cover with a clean dish towel. Place in a warm, draft-free spot for about 45 minutes to rise (an *unheated* oven is perfect). The dough will double in size.

6. Knead the dough gently for 1 minute and cut it into twelve pieces.

7. Take a section of dough and roll it in your palms to make a ball. Poke your thumbs through the center and work around to make a hole a bit larger than the size of a quarter. Repeat with the remaining sections.

8. Place the bagels on a lightly floured wooden cutting board, cover with a dish towel, and place in a warm, draft-free spot for 20 minutes.

9. Meanwhile, bring 3 quarts of water to a boil. Preheat the oven to 400°.

10. Follow the kettling and baking instructions on page 29 (steps 10 through 13).

Makes 12 bagels

5

Low-Fat, Low-Cal Feasts

Bagels are good for you! They have no cholesterol, very little fat, and more protein than other bread products, consisting solely of complex carbohydrates, water, and flavoring. And sinking your teeth into a bagel beats a boring piece of bread any day. So try these winning combinations. Then create your own healthful favorites.

Bagelberry Slam-Dunk

Enjoy these with a cup of steaming almond extract–flavored coffee.

1 cup part-skim ricotta cheese
One 10-ounce package frozen raspberries, thawed and drained
1 cup blueberries (fresh or frozen, thawed and drained)
1 tablespoon confectioners' sugar (or artificial sweetener to taste)
3 bagels, halved and toasted

33

In a blender or food processor, blend the ricotta cheese, raspberries, blueberries, and sugar. Cut toasted bagel halves in sections and dunk your way through breakfast.

Makes about 1½ cups (6 servings)

Per serving ½ bagel and ¼ cup dip: 28 g. carbohydrates; 9 g. protein; 4 g. fat; 2 mg. cholesterol; 225 mg. sodium; 183 calories

Strawberries-and-Cream Bagels

¾ cup fresh strawberries
½ cup part-skim ricotta cheese
½ teaspoon granulated sugar (or artificial sweetener to taste)
1 bagel, halved and toasted
Fresh mint (optional)

1. Mash ¼ cup strawberries and mix with ricotta cheese and sugar.

2. Blend well and spread each toasted bagel half with mixture.

3. Slice remaining strawberries and place on top of ricotta cheese.

4. Garnish with mint leaves, if desired. Serve open-face.

Makes 2 servings

Per serving: 27 g. carbohydrates; 11 g. protein; 6 g. fat; 2 mg. cholesterol; 225 mg. sodium; 205 calories

Palm Beach Salad

4 chicken breasts cooked, deboned, and cut into bite-size chunks
½ cup Kraft Free® Catalina® nonfat dressing
⅓ cup nonfat yogurt
¼ cup finely chopped celery
Salt and pepper to taste
1 tablespoon capers (optional)
4 bagels, halved

1. While chicken chunks are still warm, mix them with dressing; refrigerate for several hours or overnight.

2. Add yogurt, celery, salt, and pepper to taste, and capers, if desired. Refrigerate until ready to serve.

3. Make into bagel sandwiches or serve on salad greens with bagels on the side.

Makes 4 servings
Per serving: 49 g. carbohydrates; 46 g. protein; 7 g. fat; 109 mg. cholesterol; 762 mg. sodium; 443 calories

Gluten Maximus

Eggsactly Bagels

4 hard-boiled eggs, peeled and chopped
2 teaspoons nonfat mayonnaise
¼ cup nonfat yogurt
Salt and pepper to taste
¼ cup finely chopped celery (optional)
4 bagels, halved

Mix eggs, mayonnaise, and yogurt. Add salt and pepper to taste and celery, if desired. Spread on bagels.

Makes 4 servings
Per serving: 39 g. carbohydrates; 15 g. protein; 8 g. fat; 254 mg. cholesterol; 477 mg. sodium; 287 calories

Veggie Bagels

¾ cup 2 percent cottage cheese
⅛ cup very finely chopped radishes
⅛ cup grated green pepper
¼ cup finely chopped celery
⅛ cup grated carrots
¼ cup finely chopped scallion (spring onion)
Salt and pepper to taste
1 bagel, halved

Mash cottage cheese with a fork; add radish, green pepper, celery, carrot, scallion, and salt and pepper to taste. Spread on bagel halves.

Makes 2 servings
Per serving: 20 g. carbohydrate; 13 g. protein; 4 g. fat; 12 mg. cholesterol; 520 mg. sodium; 169 calories

The Big Dipper

One 16-ounce container 2 percent cottage cheese
1 package light powdered Italian Dressing
½ teaspoon garlic powder
1 tablespoon finely chopped onion
Bagel chips, carrot sticks, celery sticks, green and red pepper slices

Puree the cottage cheese in a food processor or blender. Fold in the seasonings. Serve with bagel chips and raw veggies for dipping.

Makes about 2 cups (8 servings)
Per ¼ serving of dip: 3 g. carbohydrates; 8 g. protein; 1 g. fat; 5 mg. cholesterol; 85 mg. sodium; 54 calories

Raisin in the Bun

½ cup 2 percent cottage cheese, mashed with a fork
1 teaspoon dark brown sugar
1 tablespoon golden raisins
1 cinnamon-raisin bagel, halved

Blend cottage cheese and brown sugar. Add raisins and mix well. Spread on bagel halves.

Makes 2 servings
Per serving: 29 g. carbohydrates; 11 g. protein; 2 g. fat; 5 mg. cholesterol; 115 mg. sodium; 177 calories

Cheese Melts

1 bagel, halved
3 slices fat-free cheese
2 thin tomato slices
Dash garlic powder
Dash black pepper

Place 1½ slices of cheese on each bagel half. Top each with a slice of tomato. Sprinkle with garlic powder and black pepper. Place in toaster oven or under broiler until cheese melts.

Makes 2 servings
Per serving: 20 g. carbohydrates; 12 g. protein; .53 g. fat; 5 mg. cholesterol; 485 mg. sodium; 138 calories

39

Bagel Eggels

¼ cup egg substitute
Seasonings to taste
Suggested toppings: your favorite brand of salsa; assorted chopped fresh veggies
  "sautéed" in water and seasoned to taste
1 bagel, halved and toasted

Scramble the egg substitute according to the package directions. Add seasonings. Spoon onto toasted bagel halves and add the topping of your choice.

Makes 1 serving
Per serving: 30 g. carbohydrates; 13 g. protein; 1 g. fat; 0 mg. cholesterol; 530 mg. sodium; 215 calories

Tuna Trimmer

1 6½-ounce can white tuna in water, drained
1 teaspoon low-fat mayonnaise
2 tablespoons nonfat yogurt
1 tablespoon finely chopped celery
1 teaspoon finely chopped onion (optional)
2 bagels, halved

Mix tuna, mayonnaise, and yogurt in a blender or food processor for a couple of seconds, or just until blended. Stir in chopped celery and onion, if desired. Divide mixture in half to make two bagel sandwiches.

Makes 2 servings
Per serving: 40 g. carbohydrates; 30 g. protein; 3 g. fat; 37 mg. cholesterol; 865 mg. sodium; 314 calories

6

Breakfast Bagels

The Big Cheese

2 bagels, halved
4½-ounces brie cheese, cut in thin slices
⅓ cup slivered almonds
Strawberry preserves

1. Preheat the oven to 350°.
2. Cover each bagel half with slices of brie.
3. Top with slivered almonds and bake on a foil-covered cookie sheet until the cheese melts.
4. Serve each half with a small spoonful of strawberry preserves.

    Makes 4 halves

Bagel Castanets

2 eggs
Freshly ground pepper to taste
2 tablespoons finely chopped onion or scallion (spring onion)
2 tablespoons finely diced green pepper
1 tablespoon finely chopped black olives
2 tablespoons chopped fresh tomato
1 ounce diced pastrami or corned beef
2 teaspoons margarine
1 bagel, halved, toasted, and spread with margarine
Bottled mild taco sauce, warmed

1. In a bowl, beat the eggs; add 2 tablespoons of water and freshly ground pepper.

2. Add chopped onion, green pepper, olives, tomato, and choice of meat. Mix well.

3. Melt the margarine in a frying pan over medium heat; add the egg mixture and scramble until done.

4. Spoon half the mixture onto each bagel half; top with taco sauce.

Makes 2 halves

For-Herring-Lovers-Only Bagels

Bagels, halved
One 8-ounce jar herring in cream sauce

Spoon herring in cream sauce onto toasted bagel halves.

Bagels Benedict

2 bagels, halved
Margarine
4 poached eggs
4 slices Monterey Jack cheese
Hollandaise Sauce (see Note)
Fresh parsley sprigs for garnish

Toast the bagel halves and spread them with margarine. Top each bagel half with a poached egg. Place a slice of cheese on each egg. Pour on Hollandaise.

Makes 4 halves

Note: To make Hollandaise Sauce: Heat ½ cup (1 stick) butter or margarine until melted and hot. Don't let it brown. Meanwhile, place 3 egg yolks, 1 tablespoon lemon juice, and a dash each of white pepper and salt in a blender and blend well. Pour in hot butter or margarine, and blend for a second or two. Makes ¾ cup sauce.

Bagel Pancakes

This is a great way to use up stale bagels. For a delightful variation, add grated apple to the batter before frying. You can freeze leftover pancakes and reheat them in a preheated 400° oven for 5 minutes (or if you're in a rush, microwave them for 1½ minutes at full power).

3 bagels
3 eggs, beaten
1½ cups milk
¼ plus ⅛ teaspoon salt
¾ teaspoon sugar
½ teaspoon vanilla
Margarine for frying
Syrup, preserves, honey, or confectioners' sugar for serving

1. Cut the bagels in small chunks and put in the blender or food processor a few at a time, grinding into crumbs.

2. Place the crumbs in a mixing bowl; add the beaten eggs, milk, salt, sugar, and vanilla. Mix very well. (Mixture will be thick.)

3. Heat the margarine on a griddle or in a large frying pan.

4. Drop the batter by heaping tablespoons into the pan (as you would regular pancakes). Flatten each with the back of the spoon.

5. Cook slowly over medium heat. You may want to add additional margarine as the pancakes cook to keep the pan from becoming dry. Cook each side until golden-brown.

6. Serve with syrup, preserves, honey, or confectioners' sugar.

Makes 12 pancakes

Note: If you want to make less than this recipe calls for, one bagel makes four pancakes. Reduce other ingredients accordingly.

"Oh, what a bagelful morning!'

Denver Bagels

4 ounces pastrami or bologna, diced
1 tablespoon finely chopped green pepper
1 tablespoon finely chopped onion
Dash pepper
Dash oregano
2 eggs, beaten with 2 tablespoons water
1 teaspoon maragine
1 bagel, halved, heated or toasted, and spread with margarine

1. Mix the pastrami with the green pepper, onion, pepper, and oregano.

2. Add the beaten egg mixture and blend well.

3. Heat the margarine in a frying pan, and scramble the eggs until firm.

4. Spoon the mixture onto the bagel halves. Serve open-face.

Makes 2 halves

46

Scrambled Bagel

1 bagel
1 egg
2 tablespoons cream cheese, cut in small pieces
1 tablespoon milk
Freshly ground pepper to taste
Salt to taste
½ teaspoon chopped scallion (spring onions) or chives (optional)
1 teaspoon butter or margarine

1. Slice off the top quarter of the bagel horizontally. Set the "top" aside.

2. Carefully scoop out the inside of the remaining bagel with your fingers and set aside the bagel bits, leaving a bagel "shell."

3. Heat the bagel shell and top in the oven; while they are warming, beat the egg with a fork or whisk.

4. Finely crumble the bagel bits you scooped out; add the crumbs to the egg.

5. Add the cream cheese, milk, pepper, salt, and scallion, if desired.

6. Melt the butter in a frying pan; scramble the egg until dry.

7. Fill the warmed bagel shell with cooked egg, and replace the bagel top.

Makes 1 serving
Note: For variety, experiment by adding shredded cheese or sliced cooked mushrooms to the egg mixture before cooking.

Bullseye Bagels

1 bagel, halved
2 teaspoons margarine
2 slices bologna
2 eggs
Freshly ground pepper

1. Toast the bagel halves lightly and spread each with ½ teaspoon margarine.

2. Meanwhile, heat the bologna slices on both sides in a frying pan; place one slice on each toasted bagel half.

3. In a separate frying pan, heat the remaining teaspoon of margarine; fry the eggs until the whites are set.

4. Sprinkle the eggs with freshly ground pepper and place one on each bagel half. Serve open-face.

Makes 2 halves

Sunrise Bagel

1 bagel, halved
1 teaspoon margarine
1 turkey-sausage patty, cooked

Heat or toast the bagel halves in a toaster or oven. Spread with margarine. Add the sausage to make a bagel sandwich.

Makes 1 serving

Fishing for Compliments

1 bagel, halved
4 ounces smoked whitefish or 2 slices sable (from your favorite deli)
4 cucumber slices
4 thin onion slices
Mayonnaise

Place fish on bottom bagel half. Top with cucumber and onion slices. Spread mayonnaise on other bagel half and place on top.

Makes 1 serving

The Traditional Bagel

1 bagel, halved
2 good-size slices smoked salmon (nova has a more delicate flavor; lox is
stronger and saltier)
2 thick tomato slices
2 thin onion slices (optional)

Spread the bagel halves with cream cheese. Top each with a slice of smoked salmon, tomato, and onion, if desired. Serve open-face or (for the adventurous) as a big sandwich.

Makes 2 halves or 1 bagel sandwich

7

Luncheon
and Dinner Bagels

Cheese Toppers

Whole bagels
Slices of your favorite cheese

Top whole bagels with slices of your favorite cheese. Place in oven or toaster oven and heat thoroughly until cheese melts.

Health Bagel

1 bagel, halved
Mayonnaise
1 small avocado, peeled and sliced
2 tablespoons alfalfa sprouts
½ cup shredded Monterey Jack cheese
2 tablespoons sesame chips, crumbled

Spread the bagel halves lightly with mayonnaise. Place the avocado slices, then alfalfa sprouts on each half. Put ½ cup of cheese on each, and top with sesame chips.

Makes 2 halves

Bagelcues

2 bagels, halved
1 pound ground beef or turkey
¼ teaspoon garlic powder
1 onion, finely chopped
1 tablespoon dark brown sugar
¼ cup barbecue sauce (any kind)

1. Preheat the oven to 375°.

2. With your fingers, scoop out the insides of the bagel halves, leaving "shells." Place the scooped-out bits in a blender and process to make fine crumbs.

3. In a frying pan over medium heat, crumble the ground meat; add the garlic powder and chopped onion, and cook thoroughly. Drain off fat.

4. Add the brown sugar, bagel crumbs, and barbecue sauce, and stir well over low heat.

5. Fill the bagel shells with the meat mixture and bake on a foil-covered cookie sheet in the preheated oven for about 15 minutes, or until heated thoroughly.

Makes 4 halves

Deli Boss Bagel

1 bagel, halved
Mustard
2 ounces pastrami
2 ounces salami
2 tablespoons chopped liver

Spread one bagel half with a thin coat of mustard. Place the pastrami and salami on top of the mustard. Spread chopped liver on other bagel half and make a sandwich.

Makes 1 serving

Bagel Soufflé

This is an absolutely scrumptious main dish or side dish! Every bite is heavenly.

¼ cup (½ stick) plus 1 tablespoon margarine or butter
4 bagels, halved
7 eggs
¼ teaspoon salt
2 cups milk
¼ teaspoon paprika
Freshly ground pepper
6 ounces Monterey Jack cheese, grated
6 ounces cheddar cheese, grated

1. Preheat the oven to 350°.

2. Grease a 2-quart casserole with 2 tablespoons of margarine or butter; cut the bagel halves into small bite-size pieces and set aside.

3. In a mixing bowl, beat together the eggs, salt, milk, paprika, and pepper.

4. Place half of the bagel cubes in the greased casserole. Mix the cheeses together; place half of the cheese mixture on top of the bagel cubes; repeat with the remaining bagel cubes and remaining cheese.

5. Carefully ladle the egg mixture into the casserole dish on top of the bagel-cheese layers, making sure to cover evenly so it seeps through. (You may want to poke holes through with a knife as you ladle.)

6. Set the casserole in the refrigerator and let it stand overnight, and until you are ready to bake it the next day.

7. Bake the casserole in preheated oven for 1 hour, or until top is golden.

Makes 8 servings

54

Bagel Slaw

2 cups shredded cabbage
4 ounces mild cheddar cheese, shredded
4 ounces Monterey Jack cheese, shredded
1 carrot, peeled and grated
¼ cup plus 1 tablespoon mayonnaise or salad dressing
Freshly ground pepper
1 bagel, cut in small bite-size cubes

1. In a mixing bowl, combine the cabbage, cheeses, and carrot.

2. Add the mayonnaise and pepper, and mix well. You can make ahead to this point.

3. Just before serving, add the bagel cubes, and mix thoroughly.

Makes 4 servings

Bagels Bourguignonne

1 cup flour
1 teaspoon seasoned salt
2 pounds pot roast, cut into bite-size cubes (or use stew beef chunks)
2 tablespoons cooking oil
1 cup beef consommé
½ cup dry white wine
1 garlic clove, minced
1 onion, finely chopped
2 carrots, peeled and julienned
2 celery stalks, finely chopped
4 bagels, halved

1. Mix the flour and seasoned salt and put in a plastic bag. Add the beef cubes and toss thoroughly to coat with flour mixture.

2. Heat the oil in a large heavy pot and brown the beef thoroughly.

3. Pour the consommé and wine over the beef.

4. Add the garlic, onion, carrot, and celery. Stir well.

5. Bring to a boil; reduce heat and let simmer for 2 to 3 hours, stirring periodically.

6. Serve over hot bagel halves.

Makes 4 servings

Bagel Burger

1 bagel, halved
¼ pound ground beef or turkey patty
¼ onion, chopped or sliced
Shredded lettuce
Bottled Thousand Island salad dressing

1. Heat or toast the bagel, or use it plain.

2. Fry the hamburger patty in the onion, and place it on one half of the bagel.

3. Top with shredded lettuce, salad dressing, and other bagel half. Then get ready to open wide!

Makes 1 serving

Bagels and Gravy

Bagels, halved
Leftover gravy from roast or bottled "home-style" gravy (see Note)

Heat the gravy in a saucepan. Spoon over heated or toasted bagel halves.

Note: Choose whatever flavor bottled gravy you prefer, or make your own. Brown gravy, chicken gravy, mushroom gravy, turkey gravy, and onion gravy are all great on bagels!

Chicken-fried Bagels

1 tablespoon cooking oil
1 egg, beaten
½ cup plus 1 tablespoon milk
1 teaspoon baking powder
¼ teaspoon salt
⅛ teaspoon pepper
¼ teaspoon paprika
¼ teaspoon garlic powder
1 cup flour
2 bagels, halved
Oil for frying
Honey or white-sauce gravy for serving

1. In a mixing bowl, beat the oil and egg with fork.

2. Add the milk, baking powder, salt, pepper, paprika, and garlic powder. Beat thoroughly with an egg beater.

3. Add the flour and beat until well mixed. Batter will be thick.

4. Place the bagel halves in the batter one at a time; using a spoon and a fork, coat both sides with batter.

5. In a large frying pan, heat about 1 inch of cooking oil. Over medium heat, fry the bagels on cut side first; when golden-brown, turn with a fork and cook on the other side until golden-brown.

6. Drain on paper towels. Serve warm, with a side dish of honey or gravy for dipping.

Makes 4 halves

58

Bagel Tuna Boats

4 bagels
One 6 ½-ounce can white tuna packed in water, drained
One 10 ½-ounce can cream of mushroom soup
2 tablespoons fresh parsley, chopped
½ of an 8-ounce can water chestnuts, drained and chopped
2 tablespoons margarine or butter

1. Preheat the oven to 375°.

2. With a serrated knife, slice a thin portion off the top of each bagel. Using your fingers, scoop out the insides of the bagels and reserve, leaving bagel "boats." Set aside.

3. Put the drained tuna in a mixing bowl and separate into fine pieces with your fingers.

4. Fold in the undiluted can of cream of mushroom soup, parsley, and water chestnuts, and mix until well blended.

5. Fill each bagel boat with a little less than a ½ cup of tuna mixture.

6. Crumble some of the scooped-out bagel bits with your fingers (or in a blender or food processor) to make fine crumbs.

7. In a frying pan, melt the margarine; add the crumbs and stir quickly, until they are light brown.

8. Sprinkle the crumbs over the tuna mixture in the bagels. Bake on a foil-covered cookie sheet for 15 to 20 minutes, or until thoroughly heated.

Makes 4 servings

Note: You can put the bagel tops and any bagel bits you didn't use for crumbs into a plastic bag and freeze for later use. You can also freeze the filled tuna boats and reheat them in a preheated 400° oven for 10 minutes.

59

Soup and Bagels

For a satisfying and fun meal, make a tureenful of your favorite hearty soup. Serve with a big basket of assorted hot, toasty buttered bagels.

Bagel Stuffing

A great way to use up stale bagels!

> *3 bagels, cut into small cubes*
> *½ cup (1 stick) margarine*
> *1 celery stalk, chopped*
> *1 medium onion, chopped*
> *8 mushrooms, chopped*
> *⅛ cup chopped fresh parsley*
> *¼ teaspoon poultry seasoning*
> *2 eggs, beaten*

1. Put the bagel cubes on a foil-covered cookie sheet, and bake in a preheated 375° oven for 15 minutes. Place the cubes in a mixing bowl.

2. In a large frying pan, melt the margarine; sauté the celery, onion, mushroom, and parsley until tender.

3. Stir in the poultry seasoning and mix thoroughly.

4. Pour the mixture over the bagel cubes in the bowl, and mix well.

5. Add the eggs and mix thoroughly. Refrigerate the stuffing mixture until chilled before stuffing poultry.

Enough stuffing for 8 pounds of poultry.

Note: To stuff a 4-pound chicken, simply cut the recipe in half. Or if you'd rather stuff yourself than the chicken, add bite-size chunks of cooked poultry to the stuffing mixture, bake in a greased casserole dish for 1 hour at 375°, and enjoy as a main course.

Beef-o-Bagels

4 bagels, halved
3 tablespoons soft margarine
3 tablespoons mustard
1 pound very lean ground beef or ground turkey
¼ cup catsup
1 onion (small or medium), chopped fine
¼ teaspoon garlic powder
¼ teaspoon seasoned salt

1. Place the bagel halves under the broiler until cut sides are toasted.

2. Meanwhile, blend the margarine and mustard.

3. Remove the bagel halves from the broiler, and spread the cut sides completely to the edges with margarine-mustard mixture. (You'll use half of the mixture for this, and the rest at the end of the recipe.)

4. In a bowl, place the ground beef, catsup, onion, garlic powder, and seasoned salt; mix well with your hands.

5. Divide the mixture into four portions. Take one portion, divide it in half again, and press it onto a bagel half, spreading it all the way to the edges. Repeat with the remaining bagel halves.

61

6. Place them under the broiler for 10 to 12 minutes, or until the meat is cooked.

7. Remove from the broiler and immediately spread the top of each with remaining margarine-mustard mixture.

Makes 8 halves

Whopper Bagel

1 bagel, halved
4 ounces corned beef (heated or cold)
¼ cup coleslaw
1 teaspoon catsup
1 tablespoon mayonnaise

Place the corned beef on one bagel half; top with coleslaw. Mix the catsup and mayonnaise; spread on other bagel half and place on top. This recipe makes one whopper of a bagel! (If you prefer, you can serve it open-face on two halves.)

Makes 1 serving

The art of being well-bread

Iron Bagel

1 bagel, halved
1 teaspoon mayonnaise or salad dressing
½ cup chopped liver
1 slice tomato

Spread each bagel half with ½ teaspoon of mayonnaise. Top with chopped liver and tomato slices, and make a bagel sandwich.

Makes 1 serving

Easy-Cheesy Bagels

1 bagel, halved
2 tablespoons cream cheese
2 ounces cheddar cheese, shredded
2 ounces Monterey Jack cheese, shredded
4 stuffed green olives, sliced

Spread each bagel half with a tablespoon of cream cheese. Mix shredded cheeses together and spoon onto halves. Top with olive slices.

Makes 2 halves

Bagel Garlic Bread

4 bagels, halved
2 tablespoons plus 2 teaspoons soft margarine or butter
Garlic powder
Oregano
Grated Parmesan

1. Preheat the oven to 375°.

2. Spread each bagel half with 1 teaspoon margarine. (Use more if desired.)

3. Generously sprinkle with garlic powder, oregano, and Parmesan.

4. Cut each half in half again vertically.

5. Place on a foil-covered cookie sheet; bake until the bagels are thoroughly heated and the tops start to brown.

   Makes 16 pieces

California Bagel Spread

Bagels, halved
One 4-ounce package cream cheese, softened
1½ tablespoons honey
⅛ cup golden raisins
1 medium carrot, peeled and grated
¼ cup chopped walnuts

Mix the cream cheese and honey. Add the raisins, carrot, and walnuts. Spread on bagels.

Makes approximately 1 cup of spread

Poorboy Bagel

1 bagel, halved
2 teaspoons mustard
2 thick salami or bologna slices
1 lettuce leaf
2 thin tomato slices

Spread the bagel halves with mustard. Place the salami slices on one half; top with lettuce leaf, tomato slices, and other bagel half.

Makes 1 serving

Kojak Bagel

1 bagel, halved
Olive oil
Shredded lettuce
4 ounces feta cheese, crumbled
2 tomato slices
2 thin onion slices
4 pitted Greek olives, sliced
2 slices of anchovies (optional)

Drizzle the bagel halves very lightly with olive oil. Place a small amount of shredded lettuce on each. Add feta cheese, and onion and tomato slices; top with sliced olives and anchovies, if desired.

Makes 2 halves

Bagel Melts

One 6½-ounce can white tuna packed in water, well drained and flaked
¼ cup mayonnaise
1 tomato, cut into cubes
1 celery stalk, chopped
2 bagels, halved
4 slices cheddar cheese

1. Preheat the broiler.

2. Mix the tuna, mayonnaise, tomato cubes, and celery until well blended. Spoon onto bagel halves. Top each half with a slice of cheddar cheese.

3. Place under the broiler, and cook until the cheese melts.

Makes 4 halves

Bagel Croutons

Here's another good recipe for using up stale bagels.

1 cup cooking oil
1 garlic clove, thinly sliced
3 bagels, cut into cubes
½ cup grated Parmesan cheese
⅛ cup dried parsley

1. Place the oil and garlic in a small bowl; let sit for 1 hour.

2. Heat the garlic oil in a large frying pan; add the bagel cubes and cook until crisp and golden-brown, tossing constantly.

3. Drain on paper towels.

4. When cool, toss the croutons with Parmesan and parsley, and add them to your favorite salad.

Makes approximately 2 cups

Chili Bagels

2 bagels, halved
One 15-ounce can chili
1 small onion, finely chopped

1. Toast the bagel halves or heat them in the oven.

2. Meanwhile, heat the chili in a saucepan.

3. Spoon the chili onto the heated bagel halves; top with chopped onion.

Makes 4 halves

Swiss Bagels

½ cup mayonnaise
1 cup diced Swiss cheese
1 teaspoon dried or 1 tablespoon freshly chopped parsley
2 bagels, halved
4 slices dill pickle (optional)

1. Preheat the oven to 375°.

2. Mix the mayonnaise, cheese, and parsley.

3. Spoon the mixture onto the bagel halves, and bake on a foil-covered cookie sheet for about 10 minutes, or until the cheese melts. Top each half with a dill pickle slice, if desired, before serving.

Makes 4 halves

69

The Winner's Circle

1 bagel, halved
2 teaspoons mayonnaise or salad dressing
1 hard-boiled egg, sliced
1 lettuce leaf
Salt and freshly ground pepper to taste.

Spread the mayonnaise on the bagel halves. Place the hard-boiled egg slices on one half, then a lettuce leaf. Sprinkle with salt and pepper to taste. Add other bagel half.

Makes 1 serving

Eggsotic Bagels

4 hard-boiled eggs, chopped
⅓ cup chopped salt-free dry-roasted peanuts
4 tablespoons mayonnaise or salad dressing
½ teaspoon mustard
Salt to taste
4 bagels, halved

Combine the chopped eggs, peanuts, mayonnaise, mustard, and salt to taste. Spoon onto four bagel halves; top with remaining halves to make sandwiches.

Makes 4 servings

Club Bagel

1 bagel, cut in thirds horizontally, as shown

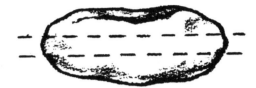

Thousand Island salad dressing
2 slices corned beef
¼ cup chopped liver
2 slices (2 ounces) turkey or chicken
2 lettuce leaves
2 slices tomato

Spread salad dressing on each layer of bagel. Place corned beef and chopped liver on one bagel layer. Top with a second bagel layer and add turkey, lettuce, and tomato. Cover with remaining third of bagel.

Makes 1 serving

Sloppy Bagels

1 pound ground beef or turkey
1 celery stalk, chopped fine
1 medium onion, chopped fine
¾ teaspoon salt
⅛ teaspoon pepper
16 ounces bottled or canned spaghetti sauce
¼ pound mushrooms, sliced thin
3 bagels, halved

1. Brown the meat in a large frying pan with the celery, onion, salt, and pepper. Drain off any fat.

2. Add the spaghetti sauce and mushrooms to the meat.

3. Simmer, uncovered, over low heat for about 10 minutes, stirring occasionally.

4. Toast the bagel halves in a toaster or oven. Spoon the mixture onto the bagel halves and serve.

Makes 6 halves

Mushroom Bagels

1 tablespoon margarine
1 cup chopped fresh mushrooms
1 small onion, chopped
¼ teaspoon dried thyme
Dash salt
1 bagel, halved
2 slices Swiss or Muenster cheese

1. Preheat the oven to 375°.

2. Sauté the mushroom and onion in margarine; stir in the thyme and salt.

3. Spoon the mixture on the bagel halves; top each with a slice of cheese.

4. Bake on a foil-covered cookie sheet for 8 to 10 minutes, or until the cheese melts.

    Makes 2 halves

The Wurst Bagel

1 jumbo cooked hot dog or knockwurst
1 bagel, halved
¼ cup sauerkraut, well drained
1 teaspoon sweet pickle relish (optional)
Mustard and catsup

Slice the hot dog in half and then into thin strips; place the strips on one bagel half. Top with sauerkraut; add relish, if desired. Spread mustard and catsup on the other bagel half and place on top.

Makes 1 serving

Bagel Mignon

4 thin packaged sandwich sub steaks, cooked according to package directions
1 bagel, halved
2 teaspoons cooking oil
1 small onion, thinly sliced
4 mushrooms, thinly sliced
¼ green pepper, thinly sliced

1. Place two thin sandwich sub steaks folded in half, on each bagel half.

2. Heat the oil in a frying pan; add the onion, mushroom, and green pepper slices, and cook until tender. Spoon the mixture onto the bagel halves.

Makes 2 halves

74

Tofu Bagel

10 ounces tofu
⅓ cup mayonnaise or salad dressing
1 tablespoon Dijon-style mustard
½ teaspoon garlic powder
¾ cup finely chopped celery
¾ cup finely chopped green pepper
1 small onion, finely chopped
1 tablespoon soy sauce
2 bagels, halved

Drain and mash the tofu. Mix it with the remaining ingredients, except the bagels, and blend well. Spoon one-fourth of the mixture onto each bagel half.

Makes 4 halves

Stir-Fried Bagels

Make your favorite recipe for vegetarian stir-fry, spoon over toasted bagel halves, top with cheese, and broil until the cheese has melted. (You can also use chicken or beef stir-fry and omit the cheese.) Delicious!

Sir Bagel Olive-ier

1 bagel, halved
Cream cheese
Stuffed green olives, sliced
Finely chopped walnuts

Spread the bagel halves generously with cream cheese. Top with stuffed green olive slices and sprinkle with walnuts.

Makes 2 halves

Tongue-in-Cheek Bagel

1 bagel, halved
Mustard
4 ounces sliced tongue
Tomato and onion slices

Spread the bagel halves with mustard. Layer tongue, tomato, and onion slices, and enjoy!

Makes 2 halves

8

Bagel Party Fare

Bagels Italiano

Bagels, halved
Margarine
Bottled Italian salad dressing
Grated Parmesan
Oregano
Dash garlic powder

1. Preheat the oven to 375°.

2. Spread the bagel halves with margarine; cut each half in four sections and place on a foil-covered cookie sheet.

3. Carefully spoon 1 teaspoon of Italian dressing on top of each section.

4. Sprinkle with Parmesan, oregano, and garlic powder.

5. Place the cookie sheet in the oven, and bake for 10 minutes, or until golden.

Rumaki Bagels

1 pound chicken livers, drained
2 tablespoons bottled teriyaki sauce
1 teaspoon sugar
One 8-ounce can water chestnuts, drained and chopped
¼ cup mayonnaise
3 bagels, halved
Fresh parsley for garnish

1. In a frying pan, cook the chicken livers with 1 tablespoon of the teriyaki sauce. As the livers cook, cut them into small pieces with a knife and fork.

2. When the livers are completely cooked, remove the pan from the heat; add the remaining 1 tablespoon teriyaki sauce, sugar, and water chestnuts. Mix thoroughly.

3. Add the mayonnaise to the mixture and blend well.

4. Spoon onto bagel halves. Cut each half in quarters. Garnish with fresh parsley, and refrigerate until serving time. You can also serve these warm: Just heat them for 10 minutes in a 375° oven. This recipe freezes beautifully.

Makes 24 portions

Fish and Chips

½ pound fish fillet (any kind), cooked
¼ cup mayonnaise or salad dressing
1 celery stalk, chopped fine
½ teaspoon Old Bay® seasoning
1 teaspoon dehydrated onion flakes or 1 tablespoon fresh chopped onion
Ground pepper to taste
One 6-ounce bag bagel chips

Crumble the fish in a mixing bowl with a fork. Add the mayonnaise and mix well. Add the chopped celery, Old Bay® seasoning, onion, and pepper, and mix until well blended. Serve as a dip with bagel chips. This is also good spooned on bagel halves, or atop shredded lettuce with a toasted bagel on the side.

Makes approximately 2 cups

Ring Around the Bagel

4 onion bagels, halved
8 ounces cream cheese
4 hard-boiled eggs, chopped fine
1 small onion, chopped fine
One 1-ounce jar caviar

1. Spread each bagel half with approximately ⅛ cup (2 tablespoons) of cream cheese, spreading completely to the edges and covering the bagel hole.

2. Using a small spoon, carefully place the chopped egg on the cream cheese, forming a circle along the outside edge of the bagel halves. Press the egg gently into the cream cheese. When you've finished, each one will look as if it has a "wreath" of chopped egg.

3. Make a circle of chopped onion inside the circle of chopped egg.

4. Place a spoonful of caviar in the center of each bagel half.

Makes 8 halves
Note: For an alternative to caviar, try flaked canned tuna or salmon

80

Bagel Tartare

¾ pound ground sirloin
½ teaspoon salt
½ teaspoon garlic powder
Ground pepper to taste
½ cup finely chopped green pepper
½ cup finely chopped onion
1 tablespoon capers (optional)
¼ cup chopped fresh parsley for garnish
4 bagels, halved and then quartered

1. Mix the sirloin, salt, garlic powder, pepper, green pepper, onion, and capers, if desired. Blend well. Place in a serving dish, and garnish with chopped parsley.

2. Serve immediately with a basket of bagel quarters. If you are not serving immediately, be sure to keep refrigerated until serving time.

Makes approximately 3 cups

Blue Bagels

½ cup mayonnaise
1 teaspoon dried or 1 tablespoon fresh chopped parsley
1 cup crumbled blue cheese
2 bagels, halved
4 tomato slices

1. Preheat the broiler

2. Mix the mayonnaise, parsley, and cheese. Spread onto bagel halves.

3. Place under the broiler until the cheese has melted.

4. Remove, and top each half with a tomato slice.

   Makes 4 halves

Bagel Coins

1 cup cooking oil
1 to 2 garlic cloves, minced (use a garlic press if you have one)
3 bagels, sliced into thin "coins" as shown, using serrated knife

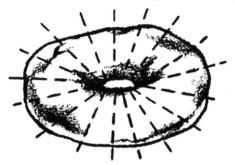

¼ cup grated Parmesan cheese
½ cup dry-roasted peanuts

1. Place the oil in a large frying pan; add the minced garlic, and stir well. (For onion-flavored coins, substitute dehydrated onion flakes for the garlic cloves.)

2. Heat the oil and add the bagel "coins." Fry until brown and crisp on both sides.

3. Drain on paper towels. When cool, place in a plastic bag with the Parmesan, and toss well.

4. Remove from the bag, mix with the peanuts, and serve. Bagel coins store well in a tightly capped jar.

Makes approximately 2½ cups

Mexicali Bagel Fondue

3 bagels, halved
4 tablespoons (½ stick) margarine
1 small onion, finely chopped
One 4-ounce can mild chopped green chilies
Flour
One 15-ounce can whole tomatoes, mashed (do not drain)
Worcestershire sauce to taste
Garlic powder to taste
12 ounces shredded cheddar cheese

1. Toast the bagel halves in a toaster or oven.

2. Cut each half into ten "chunks"; set aside.

3. In a frying pan, brown the onion in margarine; add the chilies.

4. Add enough flour to make a thick paste.

5. Over a low flame add the tomatoes, Worcestershire sauce, and garlic powder, and mix well.

6. Stir in the cheese, and blend all of the ingredients together over low heat.

7. Serve in a fondue pot with toasted bagel. (Spear chunks and dip into hot cheese mixture to coat.)

Makes approximately 3½ cups

Bagels Parmesan

2 bagels, halved
1 cup grated Parmesan cheese
½ cup mayonnaise
1 medium onion, grated
Paprika

1. Preheat the oven to 375°.

2. Mix the cheese with the mayonnaise and onion; blend well.

3. Spread onto bagel halves; sprinkle each with a dash of paprika.

4. Bake for 10 minutes, or until golden.

    Makes 4 halves

Legendary duos: Fred and Ginger, Bagels and Cream Cheese

Delhi Bagels

If you like curry, you'll love this!

½ cup soft or whipped cream cheese
¼ teaspoon plus ⅛ teaspoon curry powder
2 teaspoons chutney
⅛ cup finely chopped unsalted peanuts
1 tablespoon shredded sweetened coconut
1 bagel, halved

Mix the cream cheese, curry powder, chutney, peanuts, and coconut; blend well. Spread on bagel halves.

Makes 2 halves

Bagel Beer Fondue

1 small garlic clove, halved
¾ cup beer
1 tablespoon flour
8 ounces Swiss cheese, shredded
4 ounces sharp cheddar cheese, shredded
Freshly ground pepper
⅛ teaspoon paprika
5 bagels, cut in large bite-size chunks

1. Rub the inside of a heavy saucepan with the garlic; discard the garlic.

2. Add the beer and heat slowly.

3. Meanwhile, place the flour in a plastic bag; add the shredded cheese and shake to coat.

4. Gradually add the flour-cheese mixture to the beer. Stir constantly until thickened and bubbly, but do not boil.

5. Stir in the pepper and paprika.

6. Pour the mixture into a fondue pot, and serve with bagel chunks. (Spear chunks and dip into hot cheese mixture to coat. Add more warmed beer if the fondue becomes too thick.)

Makes approximately 2¼ cups

Inside-Out Bagels

2 bagels, halved
Dijon-style mustard
Mayonnaise
2 tablespoons sweet pickle relish (be sure to drain off juice)
20 slices bologna, cut in halves

Spread the bagel halves with mustard and mayonnaise; top each with relish. Cut each bagel half vertically into ten bite-size pieces. Wrap a half-slice of bologna around each bagel chunk, secure with a toothpick, and serve.

Makes 40 hors d'oeuvres

Sardinia Bagels

6 bagels, halved
One 8-ounce package cream cheese, softened
One 3.7-ounce tin sardines, well drained
¼ cup finely minced onion

In a small bowl, mash the sardines. Add the cream cheese and blend well. Stir in the minced onion. Serve as a spread with bagels.

Makes approximately 1¾ cups

Hummus Bagels

2 bagels, halved
One 16-ounce can chick peas (garbanzo beans), drained
½ cup tahini (sesame-seed paste)
Alfalfa sprouts
Garlic powder to taste

1. Place the chick peas in a blender or food processor, and blend until smooth.

2. Add the tahini; blend until completely mixed.

3. Add garlic powder to taste. You've just made hummus!

4. Put heaping ¼ cup of hummus on each bagel half and top with alfalfa sprouts. Or you can simply put a bowl of hummus on the table, surrounded with bagel chunks or bagel chips for dipping.

Makes 4 halves

White Pizza Bagels

4 bagels, halved
Olive oil
Garlic powder
8 ounces fontina cheese
8 teaspoons grated Parmesan cheese

1. Preheat the oven to 375°.

2. Brush each bagel half with olive oil. Sprinkle with a dash of garlic powder.

3. Top each half with 1 ounce of fontina and sprinkle each with 1 teaspoon Parmesan. Bake for 8 to 10 minutes, or until cheese is melted and top is lightly browned.

Makes 8 servings

90

For your sweet tooth . . .

Bagel Cheese Pastries

These are heavenly! Use different kinds of pie filling to make an assortment of pastries. If you'd like, you can make these a day ahead or freeze them (and thaw at room temperature before serving).

> *4 cinnamon-raisin bagels, halved*
> *One 8-ounce package cream cheese, softened (bring to room temperature)*
> *¼ cup granulated sugar*
> *⅛ teaspoon ground cinnamon*
> *2 teaspoons lemon juice*
> *1 egg*
> *1 teaspoon vanilla extract*
> *One 20-ounce can cherry-pie filling*

1. Preheat the oven to 375°.

2. With your fingers, scoop out some of the insides of the bagel halves to make shells. Freeze the scooped-out bits for other uses (such as bread crumbs or poultry stuffing).

3. In a mixing bowl, combine the cream cheese, sugar, cinnamon, lemon juice, egg, and vanilla. Beat well with an electric mixer, until the ingredients are thoroughly blended.

4. Carefully spoon the mixture into the bagel shells.

5. Bake on a foil-covered cookie sheet for 15 minutes, or until filling sets.

6. When cool, top each half with a couple of spoonfuls of cherry pie filling.

Makes 8 halves

Butterscotch Bagels

2 bagels, halved
4 teaspoons margarine or butter
1⅓ cups butterscotch chips
One 2¼-ounce package salted cashews, chopped

1. Preheat the oven to 375°.

2. Spread each bagel half with a teaspoon of margarine, and place on a foil-covered cookie sheet.

3. Top each buttered half with ⅓ cup of butterscotch chips.

4. Top with chopped cashews, and bake for 15 to 20 minutes, or until the chips melt.

   Makes 4 halves

Perfectly Pecan Bagels

3 cinnamon-raisin bagels, halved
3 eggs
½ cup dark brown sugar
1 cup light corn syrup
⅛ teaspoon salt
1 teaspoon vanilla extract
1 tablespoon margarine or butter, melted
¾ cup chopped pecans
30 pecan halves for garnish

1. Preheat the oven to 375°.

2. Scoop out the insides of the bagel halves with your fingers. Crumble the scooped-out bits, and set them aside. You will have six "shells."

3. In a mixing bowl, beat the eggs; add the brown sugar, corn syrup, salt, and vanilla. Beat well.

4. Add the melted margarine and blend.

5. Stir in the chopped pecans and crumbled bagel bits; mix thoroughly.

6. Spoon the mixture carefully into the bagel halves, and top each with five pecan halves.

7. Bake on a foil-covered cookie sheet for approximately 25 minutes, or until lightly browned.

8. Transfer to a plate to cool, or they will stick to the foil.

Makes 6 halves

Chocolate-covered Bagel Chips

12 ounces semisweet chocolate chips
3 tablespoons cooking oil
One 6-ounce bag plain bagel chips (don't buy flavored chips such as garlic,
  onion, etc.)
½ cup chopped walnuts or pecans
½ cup shredded sweetened coconut

1. Place the chocolate chips and oil in a saucepan. Over low heat, stir constantly with a wooden spoon until the chips melt and the mixture is blended thoroughly.

2. Keeping the saucepan on a very low flame, drop the bagel chips in the chocolate one at a time, turning to coat. Use a wooden spoon to make sure both sides are thoroughly coated. Spoon off the excess chocolate, and place them on a wax paper–covered cookie sheet.

3. When all of the bagel chips are coated and on wax paper, sprinkle some with coconut and some with chopped nuts. Refrigerate until the chocolate hardens. If you've used whole bagel chips, you can break them into small pieces if you'd like.

Makes enough to coat 14 whole bagel chips.

Note: Be sure to keep these in the refrigerator until serving time. (It's also a good place to hide them from chocoholics.) True chocolate lovers can use chocolate jimmies (sprinkles) in place of coconut and nuts. Multicolored jimmies are fun, too!

Chocolate-Almond Bagel Fondue

One 6-ounce package semisweet chocolate chips
2 teaspoons margarine or butter
½ cup light cream
¼ teaspoon almond extract
4 bagels, cut into bite-size chunks

1. Place the chocolate chips and margarine in a saucepan, and begin melting over low heat.

2. As the chips start to melt, gradually add the cream, stirring constantly.

3. When the chips have melted completely and the mixture is blended, add the almond extract, and mix well.

4. Pour the warmed mixture into a fondue pot set over a low flame. Serve with bite-size bagel chunks and fondue forks for dipping.

Makes 4 servings

95

The Big-Apple Bagel

Try this with a scoop of ice cream or whipped cream for an added treat.

> **5 cinnamon-raisin bagels**
> **One 21-ounce can apple-pie filling**
> **1 cup flour (all-purpose or whole-wheat graham flour)**
> **¼ cup (½ stick) soft margarine or butter**
> **2 tablespoons dark brown sugar**
> **¼ teaspoon ground cinnamon**

1. Preheat the oven to 375°.

2. Slice a thin portion off the top of each bagel, as shown.

Using your fingers, scoop out the insides to make "shells." Freeze the scooped-out bits and tops for later use.

3. Place ½ cup of pie filling in each bagel shell.

4. Place the flour, margarine, brown sugar, and cinnamon in a small bowl, and mix with a fork. Then crumble with your fingers until thoroughly blended.

5. Spoon the crumb topping over the apple-filled bagels, pressing the crumbs onto the filling. Bake on a foil-covered cookie sheet for 30 minutes, or until topping is lightly browned. Serve warm. Try this with a scoop of ice cream or whipped cream for an added treat.

Makes 5 servings

Bagel Rummy

RUM SAUCE

⅓ cup soft margarine
1 cup dark brown sugar
2 tablespoons light corn syrup
⅓ cup light cream
½ teaspoon rum extract

4 very fresh cinnamon-raisin bagels, cut in half horizontally
2 pints rum-raisin ice cream

1. Preheat oven to 375°.

2. Prepare the rum sauce: Melt the margarine over low heat. Stir in the brown sugar, corn syrup, and cream, and bring to a boil. Remove from the heat, and stir in the rum extract.

3. Heat the bagel halves in the oven until warm.

3. Remove them from the oven, and immediately place a scoop of rum-raisin ice cream on each bagel half.

4. Top with warm rum sauce.

Makes 8 servings (about 1½ cups sauce)

Berry Good Bagels

1 bagel, halved
Confectioners' sugar
1 cup blueberry, cherry, or strawberry canned pie filling
Whipped cream or dessert topping

1. Preheat oven to 375°.

2. Sprinkle the cut sides of the bagel halves lightly with sugar, and heat them in the oven until warm.

3. Spoon ½ cup of pie filling on each half.

4. Top with a generous helping of whipped cream or topping.

Makes 2 servings

Bagels Alaska

1 cinnamon-raisin bagel, halved
1 cup ice cream (any flavor—we like butter pecan)
½ cup miniature marshmallows
2 tablespoons chocolate fudge topping or syrup

1. Preheat the oven to 500°, and get ready to work fast.

2. Put ½ cup ice cream on each bagel half.

3. Press the miniature marshmallows into the ice cream.

4. Place on a foil-covered cookie sheet, and bake for 2 to 3 minutes, or until the marshmallows are lightly browned.

5. Remove from the oven, and top each half with a tablespoon of chocolate fudge topping.

6. Serve immediately, with a sharp knife and a spoon or fork.

Makes 2 servings

Coconutty Bagels

⅛ cup shredded sweetened coconut
⅛ cup chopped walnuts
1 teaspoon dark brown sugar
⅛ cup soft margarine
1 tablespoon almond brickle chips (optional)
1 bagel, halved

1. Preheat the oven to 400°.

2. Combine the coconut, chopped nuts, brown sugar, and margarine.

3. Add brickle chips, if desired. Mix well.

4. Spread on bagel halves. Bake on a foil-covered cookie sheet for 8 to 10 minutes, or until heated thoroughly. Cool for 5 minutes before serving.

Makes 2 halves

Chewy Bagel Candy

18 caramels
¼ cup plus 2 tablespoons chopped macadamia nuts
1 bagel, cut in twelfths vertically, as shown

1. Place the caramels and 2 teaspoons of water in a saucepan, and melt over low heat, stirring constantly.

2. As the caramels start to melt, add ¼ cup chopped macadamia nuts, and continue stirring over heat.

3. Remove from the heat. Quickly spear bagel chunks with fork, one at a time, and dip into caramel-nut mixture until coated on all sides; place on wax paper. Work quickly so the mixture doesn't harden. (If it does, you can reheat it over a low flame.)

4. When all of the pieces are coated, sprinkle them with the remaining 2 tablespoons of chopped nuts; press the nuts into the caramel coating.

5. Let cool, and cover with plastic wrap.

Makes 12 pieces

Cannoli Bagels

1 cup ricotta cheese (regular or part-skim)
¼ teaspoon vanilla extract
1 tablespoon plus 1 teaspoon confectioners' sugar
1 tablespoon chopped citron (or the kind of mixed assorted chopped fruits used
for fruitcake)
¼ cup semisweet chocolate chips
1 cinnamon-raisin bagel, halved
1 tablespoon chopped pistachio nuts or chopped slivered almonds

1. Place the ricotta cheese in a blender or processor; blend for a few seconds, or until creamy.

2. With a spatula, scrape the cheese into a mixing bowl. Add the vanilla and sugar; mix well.

3. Chop the citron into small bits, and add to the cheese mixture, together with the chocolate chips. Blend well.

4. Place half of the mixture on each bagel half, and sprinkle with chopped pistachio nuts or almonds.

Makes 2 servings

101

9

Children's Favorites

Buzz-Buzz Spread

1½ tablespoons honey
½ cup (1 stick) margarine or butter
2 tablespoons golden raisins
Bagels, halved and toasted

Mix the honey and margarine or butter. Add the raisins, and mix again. Spread on toasted bagel halves.

Makes about ½ cup of spread

Apple–Peanut Butter Bagels

2 bagels, halved
Soft margarine or butter
⅓ cup peanut butter
⅛ cup plus 1 tablespoon applesauce
⅛ cup finely chopped unpeeled red apple

1. Lightly spread the bagel halves with margarine.
2. Place the peanut butter and applesauce in a small bowl. Mix until smooth.
3. Stir in the chopped apple. Blend well.
4. Spread on the bagel halves.

    Makes 4 halves

PBJ Bagels

You guessed it . . . an old standby in a new shape!

Bagels, halved
Peanut butter
Jelly

Spread peanut butter and jelly on the bagel halves. Serve open-face or as a big bagel sandwich.

104

Oh-Oh French Toast

1 egg
1 tablespoon milk
¼ teaspoon vanilla extract
Dash ground cinnamon
Dash salt
¼ teaspoon sugar
1 bagel, halved
2 teaspoons margarine or butter
Confectioners' sugar

1. In a mixing bowl, combine the egg, milk, vanilla, cinnamon, salt, and sugar. Beat with a fork.

2. Pierce the tops of the bagel halves with a fork in several places, and place them in the egg mixture, cut sides down. Soak for about 5 minutes; turn to coat both sides.

3. Melt the margarine or butter in a frying pan; add the bagel halves. Cook slowly over medium heat until brown on both sides and cooked through. (The cut sides will need extra cooking time.)

4. Sprinkle with sugar, and serve open-face. Or top with blueberry or strawberry preserves, syrup, or honey.

Makes 2 halves

Circus Bagels

1 bagel, halved
4 tablespoons crunchy peanut butter
½ banana, sliced
2 teaspoons shredded sweetened coconut

Spread toasted or plain bagel halves with peanut butter. Top with banana slices, and sprinkle with coconut.

Makes 2 halves

Pizza Bagels

1 bagel, halved
¼ cup spaghetti sauce or pizza sauce
¼ teaspoon oregano
½ cup shredded mozzarella cheese

1. Preheat the oven to 375°.

2. Spread ⅛ cup spaghetti sauce on each bagel half.

3. Sprinkle oregano over the sauce, and top each half with ¼ cup of mozzarella cheese.

4. Bake on a foil-covered cookie sheet for 8 to 10 minutes, or until the cheese bubbles and begins to brown.

Makes 2 halves
Note: If you like, add any of your favorite pizza toppings before baking.

Go-Fish Bagel

1 bagel, halved
1 teaspoon mayonnaise
2 fish sticks, cooked according to package directions
1 slice American cheese
Shredded lettuce, optional

Spread the bagel halves lightly with mayonnaise. Place the fish sticks on one bagel half; add cheese. Top with shredded lettuce, if desired, and other bagel half.

Makes 2 halves

The Sugarplum Bagel

¼ cup plum preserves
¼ cup finely chopped almonds
1 bagel, halved
Confectioners' sugar

In a small bowl, mix the preserves with the almonds; spoon the mixture onto each bagel half. Sprinkle with sugar before serving.

Makes 2 halves

107

Snowball Bagels

1 cinnamon-raisin bagel, halved
Two 5-ounce cans prepared vanilla pudding
1 cup frozen nondairy whipped topping, thawed
½ cup shredded sweetened coconut

Preheat oven to 375°. Heat the bagel halves in the oven just until warmed. Spoon one can of vanilla pudding onto each bagel half. Spoon ½ cup of whipped topping on each bagel half, over the pudding. Sprinkle each with ¼ cup coconut.

Makes 2 servings

Soup Sponges

Heat up your children's favorite hearty soup, like cream of chicken or cheddar-cheese. Serve with toasted bagels spread with margarine. Dipping crusty bagels into thick hearty soup is a delicious way to enjoy them both!

Choca-Lotta-Peanut-Butta Bagels

Bagels
Canned ready-to-spread chocolate frosting
Peanut butter (smooth or crunchy)
Chopped peanuts

1. Cut each bagel in thirds, horizontally, as shown.

2. Spread one layer with peanut butter; then place a second layer on top, and spread that with peanut butter.

3. Add the third layer. Spread the top with chocolate frosting, and sprinkle on chopped peanuts.

Monkey Bagels

Cinnamon-raisin bagels, halved
1 tablespoon honey
1 ripe banana, mashed
¾ cup whipped cream cheese
¼ cup finely chopped pecans

Mix the honey, banana, cream cheese, and nuts until well blended. Use as a spread on bagel halves or as a dip for dunking.

Makes 1 cup of spread

Honey Dips

1 bagel, halved and toasted
Butter or margarine
Honey

Butter the toasted bagel halves. Serve with a small bowl of honey for dipping.

Introducing the world's first four-ring circus

Frosty the Bagel

Bagels, halved
1 can ready-to-spread chocolate frosting
Colored jimmies (sprinkles)

Frost the cut side of one half of a bagel. Replace the second half, and spread frosting on top. Sprinkle with jimmies.

Pineapple-Cream Bagels

½ cup whipped cream cheese or ricotta cheese
2 teaspoons dark brown sugar
¼ cup finely chopped pecans
1 pineapple ring, chopped, drained on paper towels
1 bagel, halved
2 whole pineapple rings, drained on paper towels

Combine the cream cheese or ricotta cheese, brown sugar, pecans, and chopped pineapple; mix thoroughly. Spread onto bagel halves, and top each with a whole pineapple ring.

Makes 2 halves

112

Circle Burgers

4 bagels, halved
1 egg
½ cup water
¾ cup uncooked oatmeal
1 teaspoon salt
3 tablespoons catsup
1 pound lean ground beef or turkey

1. Preheat the oven to 375°.

2. Mix all of the ingredients except the bagels.

3. Spread the mixture on each bagel half, leaving a hole in the middle.

4. Bake for 40 minutes, or until filling is cooked thoroughly.

   Makes 8 servings

Grilled-Cheese Bagel

1 bagel, halved
1 teaspoon margarine
Two 1-ounce slices cheese

Turn on broiler or preheat oven to 375°. Spread each bagel half with margarine. Place a slice of cheese on each. Place in the toaster oven or under the broiler, and cook until the cheese melts. Put two bagel halves together for an extra-cheesy sandwich.

Makes 2 halves

Cinnabagels

2 bagels, halved and toasted
2 teaspoons margarine
Cinnamon-sugar mixture (1 tablespoon sugar and
½ teaspoon ground cinnamon)

Spread the hot toasted bagel halves with margarine. Sprinkle with cinnamon-sugar mixture.

Makes 4 halves

Apple-Butter Bagels

Bagels, halved and toasted
Margarine
Apple butter
Finely chopped almonds (optional)

Spread the hot toasted bagel halves with margarine. Top with generous spoonfuls of apple butter. Sprinkle with finely chopped almonds, if desired.

A Bagel Glossary

Bagel Chips: Very thin bagel slices that have been baked until they are crunchy-crisp; a bagel baker's solution for giving day-old bagels new life; use with dips, soups, or simply as is.

Bagelettes: Miniature bagels that are wonderful at parties, or for children at mealtime and snacktime; they also make great teething rings.

Bagel Flavors: Once available only plain, bagels now exist in a dizzying variety of flavors: onion, garlic, egg, poppy seed, sesame seed, coarse salt, pumpernickel, rye, cinnamon-raisin, wheat, honey-wheat, banana-nut, cheese, carrot, English muffin, cherry, raspberry, blueberry, chocolate chip, and, in California, even jalapeño.

Bagel Holes: There are none; unlike doughnut holes, bagels holes really are *holes*. There is no dough left over in the bagel-shaping process, whether manual or automated. When bagels are made by hand, the dough is either formed into ropes and pressed together at the ends, or shaped into balls with the centers pushed through and widened with the fingers.

Bagelmania: A physiological condition that occurs when you're driving home in the car with a bag of hot bagels, fresh from the bakery; usually results in eating several before you get home. Side effects: telltale crumbs that stick to your coat or jacket, especially if you're wearing corduroy.

Bagel Maven: Someone who thinks he or she is an expert on bagels; frequently from New York or even New Jersey.

Bagel Purist: A traditionalist who feels that anything other than a plain bagel with a *shmear* of cream cheese is a fraud.

Black 'n' Whites: Bagels made with a combination of pumpernickel and plain doughs.

Cement Doughnut: Term of endearment used to describe bagels; considered acceptable if a bagel lover says it, heresy if it comes from anyone else.

Cheese Bagels: A thin-skinned whole bagel shell completely filled with a blend of blintze-like cheeses; a favorite of Canadians.

E. T. Bagels: Also called "Everything Bagels," they have many different toppings, typically sesame seeds, poppy seeds, onion, garlic, and coarse salt. A great combo!

Kettling: The stage in the bagel-making process in which the formed bagels are boiled just prior to being baked.

L. A. Bagels: Not a basketball term; bagels that are definitely mellower, with a lighter, less dense consistency, than their New York cousins; usually made with more yeast.

New York Bagels: Considered the apotheosis of "bageldom" and the standard by which all other bagels should be judged, because the U.S. bagel industry had its roots in New York City; it is also believed that the excellent quality of New York water enhances both the flavor and crust of these bagels.

Shmear: a generous spread of cream cheese atop a bagel.

Special-Occasion Party Bagels: When it comes to holidays, you can buy green bagels for St. Patrick's Day, pink ones for Valentine's Day, even red (cherry), white (plain), and blue (blueberry) bagels for Independence Day. For parties, order a 16-inch bagel from a bagel bakery and have it filled with lox, cream cheese, whitefish, tomatoes, cheese, or meats and coleslaw—whatever combo you desire. Slice it up and serve it to a crowd! Or order a 16-inch cinnamon-raisin bagel, write HAPPY BIRTHDAY in icing on the top, add candles, and you have the perfect "birthday cake" for any bagel lover.

Steaming: A mass-production process in which the kettling step is bypassed, and instead, racks of bagels are rolled into upright steam-injected ovens prior to baking; results in a softer bagel.

Water Bagel: A term that actually describes all bagels, since all are boiled in water or steamed in water prior to baking; the boiling process is also referred to as "kettling."

Bagel Buyer's Directory

Wherever you are, you're never far from a bagel bakery! Here's the most complete list available. No self-respecting bagel lover should be without it.

ALABAMA

The Bagel Factory
3118 Cahaba Heights Plaza
Birmingham, AL 35243
205-969-0000

Bagel Place
4925 University Dr. NW
Huntsville, AL 35816
205-830-5600

ALASKA

The Bagel Deli
Old Seward & Hoffman Rd.
Anchorage, AK 99511
907-345-3850

Thee Bakery
3020 Minnesota Dr.
Anchorage, AK 99503
907-276-7606

ARIZONA

B J's Bagel Works
6350 E. Main St.
Mesa, AZ 85205
602-985-4128

Bagel Baker
1919 W. North Ln.
Phoenix, AZ 85021
602-943-4373

Chompie's
10858 N. 32nd St.
Phoenix, AZ 85028
602-971-8010

Hot Bagel Bakery Restaurants
7114 E. Broadway Blvd.
Tucson, AZ 85710
602-296-4164

Hot Bagel Bakery Restaurants
2829 E. Speedway Blvd.
Tucson, AZ 85716
602-795-0742

Bagelry Restaurant
2575 N. Campbell Ave.
Tucson, AZ 85719
602-881-6674

Bagelry Restaurant
831 N. Park Ave.
Tucson, AZ 85719
602-882-6674

CALIFORNIA

Just Bagels
5859 Kanan Rd.
Agoura Hills, CA 91301
818-889-7812

Boogie Woogie Bagel Boy
1227 Park St.
Alameda, CA 94501
510-523-8979

Los Bagels Company
1061 I St.
Arcata, CA 95521
707-822-3150

Big Apple Bagels
8793 Plata Ln.
Atascadero, CA 93422
805-461-0263

The Bagelry
3604 Ming Ave.
Bakersfield, CA 93309
805-831-5427

Noah's New York Bagels
3170 College Ave.
Berkeley, CA 94705
510-654-0944

Brother's Bagel Factory
1218 Santa Fe Ave.
Berkeley, CA 94706
510-527-0272

Brother's Bagel Factory
1281 Gilman St.
Berkeley, CA 94706
510-524-3104

Noah's New York Bagels
1883 Solano Ave.
Berkeley, CA 94707
510-525-4447

Brother's Bagel Factory
1469 Shattuck Ave.
Berkeley, CA 94709
510-649-9422

Bagel Depot
578 Bonanza Trail
Big Bear Lake, CA 92315
714-866-6096

House of Bagels
260 Lorton Ave.
Burlingame, CA 94010
415-343-3633

Sherman Plaza Bakery
22910 Vanowen St.
Canoga Park, CA 91307
818-883-1918

Santa Clarita Valley Bagel
19372 Soledad Rd.
Canyon Country, CA 91351
805-298-7002

New York Bagel Factory
1009 N. Cindy Ln.
Carpinteria, CA 93013
805-566-6653

Southland Bakery
1174 Sandhill Ave.
Carson, CA 90746
310-763-7636

Florentine Bakery
10370 Mason Ave.
Chatsworth, CA 91311
818-998-2471

Bagels By The Bay
1201 1st St.
Coronado, CA 92118
619-437-1567

Bagels Etc.
250 E. 17th St.
Costa Mesa, CA 92627
714-645-7877

Bagel Heaven
333 E. 17th Pl.
Costa Mesa, CA 92627
714-642-4567

Bagel Works
21269 Stevens Creek Blvd. #6
Cupertino, CA 95014
408-446-2772

Bagels Plus
223B Serramonte Center
Daly City, CA 94015
415-756-1404

House of Bagels
115 Town & Country Dr. #F
Danville, CA 94526
510-838-8508

Beau Bagels
1760 E. 8th St.
Davis, CA 95616
916-753-4700

Beau Bagels
1949 5th St. #103
Davis, CA 95616
916-758-7922

Bagel Bakery of Dublin
7168 Regional St.
Dublin, CA 94568
510-829-5434

Bagel Barons
24331 Muirlands Blvd.
El Toro, CA 92630
714-588-7279

Noah's New York Bagels
4240 Hollis
Emeryville, CA 94608
510-655-6624

Garden State Bagels
191 N. El Camino Real
Encinitas, CA 92024
619-942-2435

Holey Roll Bagel
358 W. El Norte Pkwy.
Escondido, CA 92026
619-743-2565

Los Bagels Company
321 3rd St.
Eureka, CA 95501
707-442-8525

Bagels And
3782 Mowry Ave.
Fremont, CA 94538
510-796-9339

Fresno Bagel Company
7739 N. 1st St.
Fresno, CA 93720
209-436-8132

New York Bagel Factory
5674 Calle Real
Goleta, CA 93117
805-683-2392

Bagels R Bagels
14665 Bear Valley Rd.
Hesperia, CA 92345
619-244-1788

Baltimore Bagel
7523 Fay Ave.
La Jolla, CA 92037
619-456-0716

Baltimore Bagel
4150 Regents Park Row
La Jolla, CA 92037
619-587-1136

I Love Bagels
281 Crown Valley Pkwy.
Laguna Niguel, CA 92677
714-831-3300

Eastside Bagel & Deli
2789 W. Avenue L
Lancaster, CA 93536
805-722-1999

Bagels Galore
1943 Pacific Coast Hwy.
Lomita, CA 90717
310-326-3699

Bagel Bistro
4105 Atlantic Ave.
Long Beach, CA 90807
310-490-9905

Kotch's Bakery
8583 W. Pico Blvd.
Los Angeles, CA 90035
310-289-9820

Bagel Broker
7825 Beverly Blvd.
Los Angeles, CA 90036
213-931-1258

New York Bagel
11640 San Vicente Blvd.
Los Angeles, CA 90049
213-820-1050

Brooklyn Bagel Bakery
2217 W. Beverly Blvd.
Los Angeles, CA 90057
213-413-4114

Bagelmania
39840 Los Alamos Rd.
Murrieta, CA 92562
714-698-1234

Bagel Adventure
1408 Clay St.
Napa, CA 94559
707-353-7143

East Side Bagel & Deli
9161 Reseda Blvd.
Northridge, CA 91324
818-886-8736

Piedmont Bagel Bakery
4301 Piedmont Ave.
Oakland, CA 94611
510-654-5211

Everybody's Bagel Company
5725 E. 14th St.
Oakland, CA 94621
510-533-8235

Baltimore Bagel
3837 Plaza Dr.
Oceanside, CA 92056
619-726-7700

Bagel Heaven
3935 Mission Ave.
Oceanside, CA 92054
619-721-1501

Brodsky's Bagels
73131 Country Club Dr.
Palm Desert, CA 92260
619-341-0777

Brodsky's Bagels
777 E. Tahquitz Way
Palm Springs, CA 92262
619-320-0300

Brodsky's Bagels
210 E. Arenas Rd.
Palm Springs, CA 92262
619-322-4353

Smoketree Bagel Bakery & Deli
1775 E. Palm Canyon Dr.
Palm Springs, CA 92264
619-327-5443

Bagel Works
129 Lytton Ave.
Palo Alto, CA 94301
415-323-4887

Bagel Works
642 Ramona
Palo Alto, CA 94301
415-328-5429

House of Bagels
220 Hamilton Ave.
Palo Alto, CA 94301
415-323-8474

Goldstein's Bagel Bakery
86 W. Colorado Blvd.
Pasadena, CA 91105
818-792-2435

Such A Bagel & Gourmet Coffees
719 W. Channel Islands
Port Hueneme, CA 93041
805-985-1554

Bagel Den Bakery
2658 Bechelli Ln.
Redding, CA 96002
916-223-2485

Redding French Bakery
1561 E. Cypress Ave.
Redding, CA 96002
916-222-0787

Bagels Galore
1870 S. Pacific Coast Hwy.
Redondo Beach, CA 90277
310-316-3699

Bagel Works
2331 Spring St.
Redwood City, CA 94063
415-366-6923

Lox, Stock & Bagel
5225 Canyon Crest Dr.
Riverside, CA 92507
714-781-0310

Water Bagel Company
1451 Southwest Blvd.
Rohnert Park, CA 94928
707-664-9908

Bayer's Bagel Bakery
2701 Lake Tahoe Blvd.
S. Lake Tahoe, CA 96150
916-541-7882

Cream Puff Bakery
Crescent V Shopping Center
S. Lake Tahoe, CA 96150
916-544-2141

Bagful of Bagels, Inc.
1607 10th St.
Sacramento, CA 95814
916-446-6010

New York Bagel Boys
6260 Folsom Blvd.
Sacramento, CA 95819
916-739-6540

Bagful of Bagels
6260 Belleau Wood Ln.
Sacramento, CA 95822
916-424-3921

New York Bagel Boys
9131 Kiefer Blvd.
Sacramento, CA 95826
916-366-3416

Bagel Biz
7485 Rush River Dr.
Sacramento, CA 95831
916-422-4357

House of Bagels
870 Industrial Rd.
San Carlos, CA 94070
415-595-4700

Baltimore Bagel
420 Robinson Ave.
San Diego, CA 92103
619-295-1510

Baltimore Bagel
7007 Carroll Rd.
San Diego, CA 92121
619-554-1804

Baltimore Bagel
15721 Bernardo Heights Pkwy.
San Diego, CA 92128
619-451-6106

Baltimore Bagel
1772 Garnet Ave.
San Diego, CA 92109
619-272-9321

Bubby's Bagels
1011 23rd St.
San Diego, CA 92102
619-233-8207

Bagelicious
3704 Voltaire St.
San Diego, CA 92107
619-223-4788

Greatest Bagel Company
824 Camino Del Rio N
San Diego, CA 92108
619-298-7693

Superbagels
395 The Concourse
San Diego, CA 92115
619-583-9331

Baltimore Bagel
3545 Del Mar Heights Rd.
San Diego, CA 92130
619-792-7848

The Bagelry
2134 Polk St.
San Francisco, CA 94109
415-441-3003

Holey Bagel
3872 24th St.
San Francisco, CA 94114
415-647-3334

The Bagelry
4416 18th St.
San Francisco, CA 94114
415-863-0292

Holey Bagel
1206 Masonic Ave.
San Francisco, CA 94117
415-626-9111

Holey Bagel
3218 Fillmore St.
San Francisco, CA 94123
415-922-1955

Broadway Bagels
1584 Branham Ln.
San Jose, CA 95118
408-987-2245

Bagels & Deli Cafe
1712 Meridian Ave.
San Jose, CA 95125
408-264-6000

Bagel Works
5241 Prospect Rd.
San Jose, CA 95129
408-255-2321

Bagel Basket
1275 Piedmont Rd.
San Jose, CA 95132
408-272-5311

Boston Bagel
1127 Broad St.
San Luis Obispo, CA 93401
805-541-5134

Bagels Galore
28362 S. Western Ave.
San Pedro, CA 90732
310-514-3699

Marin Bagel Co.
1560 4th St.
San Rafael, CA 94901
415-457-8127

Bagel Place
1310 E. Borchard Ave.
Santa Ana, CA 92705
714-547-0787

Manhattan Bagel
1231 State St.
Santa Barbara, CA 93101
805-966-5902

Grateful Bagel
404 Mendocino Ave. #A
Santa Rosa, CA 95401
707-528-9080

Grateful Bagel
2700 Yulupa Ave.
Santa Rosa, CA 95405
707-571-8553

Broadway Bagels
12840 S. Saratoga Sunnyvale Rd.
Saratoga, CA 95070
408-867-6834

Grateful Bagel
300 S. Main St.
Sebastopol, CA 95472
707-829-5220

Bagel Factory
4454 Van Nuys Blvd.
Sherman Oaks, CA 91403
818-986-4675

Hot Bagels & Deli
4373 Woodman Ave.
Sherman Oaks, CA 91423
818-986-3121

Bagel Boys
2870 Cochran Ave.
Simi Valley, CA 93065
805-581-1739

Homegrown Baking Co.
122 W. Napa St.
Sonoma, CA 95476
707-996-0166

Bagel Express
1465 W. March Ln.
Stockton, CA 95207
209-952-2435

Bagel Kitchen
609 Porter Ave.
Stockton, CA 95207
209-478-9014

House of Bagels
1681 Hollenbeck Ave.
Sunnyvale, CA 94087
408-245-0311

Hot Bagels & Deli
19325 Ventura Blvd.
Tarzana, CA 91356
818-996-4674

Bagels & Cream
27468 Ynez Rd.
Temecula, CA 92591
714-694-8887

Bagel Junction
428 E. Main St.
Turlock, CA 95380
209-632-2435

Western Bagel
506 E. 1st St.
Tustin, CA 92680
714-730-0611

Western Bagel
23170 W. Valencia Blvd.
Valencia, CA 91355
805-254-1287

Western Bagel
7814 N. Sepulveda Blvd.
Van Nuys, CA 91405
818-786-5847

Bagel King
1686 Locust St.
Walnut Creek, CA 94596
510-938-5464

Phil A Bagel
2909 Ygnacio Valley Rd.
Walnut Creek, CA 94598
510-935-7445

Perfect Bagel
11300 W. Olympic Blvd.
West Los Angeles, CA 90064
310-478-2211

Western Bagel
3825 E. Thousand Oaks Blvd.
Westlake Village, CA 91362
805-496-0344

Western Bagel
21833 Ventura Blvd.
Woodland Hills, CA 91364
805-707-1469

COLORADO

The Bagel Nook
6480 Wadsworth Blvd.
Arvada, CO 80003
303-431-6311

The Bagel Bakery
2515 49th St.
Boulder, CO 80301
303-447-9290

Lots A Bagels
445 E. Cheyenne Mountain Blvd.
Colorado Springs, CO 80906
719-540-9096

New York Bagel Boys
6449 E. Hampden Ave.
Denver, CO 80222
303-759-2212

Bagel Store
942 S. Monaco Pkwy.
Denver, CO 80224
303-388-2648

The Bagel Deli
6217 E. 14th St.
Denver, CO 80220
303-322-0350

Ace Baking Company
1803 E. 58th
Denver, CO 80216
303-296-7482

The Bagelman
633 S. College Ave.
Fort Collins, CO 80524
303-482-4417

The Bagel Nook South
7175 W. Jefferson Ave.
Lakewood, CO 80215
303-988-5926

Agnes' Very Very
1106 N. Boise Ave.
Loveland, CO 80537
303-669-7597

CONNECTICUT

Bagel King
3550 Main St.
Bridgeport, CT 06606
203-374-4868

Bagelman II
14 Candlewood Lake Rd.
Brookfield, CT 06804
203-775-4005

Bagelman Inc.
39-B Mill Plain Rd.
Danbury, CT 06811
203-748-2464

Zaro's Bakery
7 Backus Ave.
Danbury, CT 06810
203-798-9546

Guilford Gourmet Bagel
23 Water St.
Guilford, CT 06437
203-458-2161

H. Lender & Sons Restaurant
2400 Dixwell Ave.
Hamden, CT 06514
203-248-4564

Abel's Kosher Deli
2100 Dixwell Ave.
Hamden, CT 06514
203-281-3434

The Bagel Connection
1408 Whalley Ave.
New Haven, CT 06515
203-387-1455

The Bagel Connection
61 Grove St.
New Haven, CT 06511
203-782-1441

New York Bagels & Deli
172 York
New Haven, CT 06511
203-773-3089

Bagel King
250 Westport Ave.
Norwalk, CT 06851
203-846-2633

Not Just Bagels
607 Main Ave.
Norwalk, CT 06851
203-846-4414

The Bagel Coffee Shop
327 Central Ave.
Norwich, CT 06360
203-889-0423

Clown Gallery Bakery
47 Town St.
Norwich, CT 06360
203-887-6034

Kinders Fresh Bagel Restaurant
175 Boston Post Rd.
Orange, CT 06477
203-795-3549

H. Lender & Sons Restaurant
175 Boston Post Rd.
Orange, CT 06477
203-795-3549

What-A-Bagel
463 Elm
Stamford, CT 06902
203-324-4058

Lizsue Bagels
63 High Ridge Rd.
Stamford, CT 06905
203-323-4611

Brooklyn Baking Company
8 John St.
Waterbury, CT 06708
203-574-9198

Zaro's Bake Shop
413 Post Rd. E
Westport, CT 06880
203-222-9696

The Yalesville Bakery
8 Chapel Square
Yalesville, CT 06492
203-265-7522

DELAWARE

New York Bagel & Bake
621 College Square
Newark, DE 19711
302-453-1362

Bagels & Donuts
2507 W. 6th St.
Wilmington, DE 19805
302-571-8148

Bagels & Donuts
1901 Pennsylvania Ave.
Wilmington, DE 19806
302-652-7960

Max's Bagel Cafe
4528 Kirkwood Hwy.
Wilmington, DE 19808
302-999-1517

Bagels & Donuts
1737 Marsh Rd.
Wilmington, DE 19810
302-478-9016

DISTRICT OF COLUMBIA

Chesapeake Bagel Bakery
215 Pennsylvania Ave., SE
Washington, DC 20003
202-546-0994

Bagels Etc.
1825 I St., NW
Washington, DC 20006
202-429-0700

Chesapeake Bagel Bakery
818 18th St., NW
Washington, DC 20006
202-775-4690

Georgetown Bagelry
3245 M St. NW
Washington, DC 20007
202-965-1011

Chesapeake Bagel Bakery
1636 Connecticut Ave., NW
Washington, DC 20009
202-328-7985

Booeymonger Restaurant
5252 Wisconsin Ave., NW
Washington, DC 20015
202-686-5805

Chesapeake Bagel Bakery
4000 Wisconsin Ave., NW
Washington, DC 20016
202-966-8866

Bagels Etc.
2122 P St., NW
Washington, DC 20037
202-466-7171

Whatsa Bagel
3513 Connecticut Ave., NW
Washington, DC 20008
202-966-8990

Toojay's
4620 Wisconsin Ave., NW
Washington, DC 20016
202-686-1989

FLORIDA

Bagel King Bakery & Deli
910 Sand Lake Rd.
Altamonte Springs, FL 32714
407-774-1797

Boca Bagel
7122 Beracasa Way
Boca Raton, FL 33433
407-368-8525

Boca Grove Bagel
21055 Jog Rd.
Boca Raton, FL 33433
407-483-5555

Nestor's at Bageland
7050 W. Palmetto Park Rd.
Boca Raton, FL 33433
407-391-0999

Bagel Tree
9080 Kimberly Blvd. #810
Boca Raton, FL 33434
407-487-9500

Bagel Break
1389 W. Palmetto Park Rd.
Boca Raton, FL 33486
407-395-5900

Toojay's
5030 Champion Blvd.
Boca Raton, FL 33496
407-241-5903

Rosen's Bagel Factory
5866 14th St. W
Bradenton, FL 34207
813-753-2710

Brandon Bagels
118 E. Bloomingdale Ave.
Brandon, FL 33511
813-654-9672

Long Island Bagels
11206 Spring Hill Dr.
Brooksville, FL 34609
904-686-6441

Bagel Empire
13162 Cortez Blvd.
Brooksville, FL 34613
904-596-1629

Corey's Bagels
6710 N. Atlantic Ave.
Cape Canaveral, FL 32920
407-868-0088

Corey's Bagels of Clearwater
26976 U.S. Hwy. 19 N
Clearwater, FL 34621
813-791-4663

New York Bagel Boys
2566 N. McMullen Booth Rd. #E
Clearwater, FL 34621
813-797-9891

Tasty Fresh Donuts
28798 Hwy. 19 N
Clearwater, FL 34621
813-791-6180

New York Bagel Boys
Clearwater Mall
Clearwater, FL 34624
813-799-4657

Clearwater Bagels
1871 Gulf To Bay Blvd.
Clearwater, FL 34625
813-446-7631

Bagel Hut
4877 Coconut Creek Pkwy.
Coconut Creek, FL 33063
305-977-3866

Bageland of Coral Springs
8188 Wiles Rd.
Coral Springs, FL 33067
305-752-4488

Delray Bagel
14812 Military Trail
Delray Beach, FL 33484
407-498-2888

Royal Palm Restaurant
3517 Davie Blvd.
Fort Lauderdale, FL 33312
305-587-7107

Antonio's Coffee Shop
5446 N.W. 19th St.
Fort Lauderdale, FL 33313
305-486-3137

Bagelhaven
5561 W. Oakland Park Blvd.
Fort Lauderdale, FL 33313
305-484-5062

Bagelmania
7362 W. Commercial Blvd.
Fort Lauderdale, FL 33319
305-748-5088

Healthy Bagel Restaurant
1755 N. University Dr.
Fort Lauderdale, FL 33322
305-475-0606

Hello Bagel
10031 Sunset Strip
Fort Lauderdale, FL 33322
305-746-9996

Busy Bagel
8500 W. State Rd. 84
Fort Lauderdale, FL 33324
305-472-1695

Offerdahl Bagel Gourmet
1164 Weston Rd.
Fort Lauderdale, FL 33326
305-384-6479

Sam's Bagel Club
3464 N. University Dr.
Fort Lauderdale, FL 33351
305-749-0009

Mac-Donuts
3412 S. Cleveland Ave.
Fort Myers, FL 33901
813-939-7989

Lox, Stox & Bagels
7101 Cypress Lake Dr. #61
Fort Myers, FL 33907
813-482-7711

Miami Connection Bagel & Deli
11506 S. Cleveland Ave.
Fort Myers, FL 33907
813-936-3811

Bagelville Deli
1245 W. University Ave.
Gainesville, FL 32601
904-376-0000

Bagels Unlimited
1620 W. University Ave.
Gainesville, FL 32603
904-376-6743

Bagels Unlimited
2124 S.W. 34th St.
Gainesville, FL 32608
904-372-7006

Sage Bagel & Appetizer Shop
800 E. Hallandale Beach Blvd.
Hallandale, FL 33009
305-456-7499

Ronnie's Bagel Place
2649 Hollywood Blvd.
Hollywood, FL 33020
305-921-9483

Hole in the Wall
103 Courthouse Sq.
Inverness, FL 32650
904-344-0053

Bagel Time
19 University Blvd. N
Jacksonville, FL 32211
904-724-7660

Bagel Time II
2294 Mayport Rd.
Jacksonville, FL 32233
904-249-2684

Bagels
9810 Baymeadows Rd.
Jacksonville, FL 32256
904-642-3537

Schmagel's Bagels
9850 San Jose Blvd. #1
Jacksonville, FL 32257
904-268-5273

Bagel Break Restaurant
1864 NE Jensen Beach Blvd.
Jensen Beach, FL 34957
407-334-0960

Toojay's
4050 U.S. Hwy. 1
Jupiter, FL 33458
407-627-5555

Bagel Palace
7364 Lake Worth Rd.
Lake Worth, FL 33467
407-964-9849

Toojay's Bakery
419 Lake Ave.
Lake Worth, FL 33460
407-585-3305

House Of Bagels
13469 Belcher Rd. S
Largo, FL 34641
813-531-9823

Bagel Nosh
2221 N. State Rd. 7
Lauderhill, FL 33313
305-484-4373

Best Bagels
972 State Rd. 434 W
Longwood, FL 32750
407-831-5220

Bagels Galore
7256 W. Atlantic Blvd.
Margate, FL 33063
305-979-1900

Bageland
5379 W. Atlantic Blvd.
Margate, FL 33063
305-972-0606

Corey's Bagels at Sunrise
4000 S. Babcock St.
Melbourne, FL 32901
407-729-4281

Corey's Bagels
727 Columbus Ave.
Melbourne, FL 32901
407-951-3696

Bagels Etc.
3066 Lake Washington Rd.
Melbourne, FL 32934
407-255-2398

Corey's Bagels
694 N. Wickham Rd.
Melbourne, FL 32935
407-255-0161

Beach Side Bagels
252 E. Eau Gallie Blvd.
Melbourne, FL 32937
407-773-3450

Corey's Bagels at Suntree
7025 N. Wickham Rd. #113A
Melbourne, FL 32940
407-255-0991

Frank's Bagel Nook
125 N. Banana River Dr.
Merritt Island, FL 32952
407-452-6501

Bagel Emporium
401 Biscayne Blvd.
Miami, FL 33132
305-577-4404

Bagels & Donuts
1736 79th St.
Miami, FL 33141
305-864-0430

Bagel Emporium
1238 S. Dixie Hwy.
Miami, FL 33146
305-666-9519

Poppyseed's Bagel Bakery
17170 Collins Ave.
Miami, FL 33160
305-949-9131

Bagels & Company
11064 Biscayne Blvd.
Miami, FL 33161
305-892-2435

Bagel Hole Bakery
8859 S.W. 107th Ave.
Miami, FL 33176
305-271-3880

House of Bagels
14449 S. Dixie Hwy.
Miami, FL 33176
305-251-6540

Lots of Lox Deli
14995 S. Dixie Hwy.
Miami, FL 33176
305-252-2010

Bagel Bar
18515 N.E. 18th Ave.
Miami, FL 33179
305-932-3314

Bagel Garden
12886 Biscayne Blvd.
Miami, FL 33181
305-895-1144

Broadway Bagels
13854 N. Kendall Dr.
Miami, FL 33186
305-385-0790

Beach Bagel Bakeries
1019 5th St.
Miami Beach, FL 33139
305-672-8230

A-1 Bagels
6913 Miramar Pkwy.
Miramar, FL 33023
305-964-9843

Bageland
4932 Hwy. 19 N
New Port Ritchey, FL 34652
813-841-6033

Real Bagels
7429 Hwy. 19N
New Port Ritchey, FL 34652
813-842-4981

Bagel King
9041 Little Rd.
New Port Ritchey, FL 34654
813-863-2822

Bagel Delite
1351 S. State Rd. 7
North Lauderdale, FL 33068
305-973-3294

Bagel Place
4004 S. Semoran Blvd.
Orlando, FL 32822
407-380-9296

Bagel Port
1700 Babcock St. NE #24
Palm Bay, FL 32905
407-728-3912

Toojay's
313 Poinciana Plaza
Palm Beach, FL 33480
407-659-7232

Toojay's
4084 P.G.A. Blvd.
Palm Beach Gardens, FL 33410
407-622-8131

Bagel Outlet & Deli
33855 Highway 19 N
Palm Harbor, FL 34684
813-785-9297

Bagel Go Round
1696 S. Congress Ave.
Palm Springs, FL 33462
407-439-2840

Bagel Chai
7976 Pines Blvd.
Pembroke Pines, FL 33024
305-987-8605

Bagelmania Restaurant
7849 Pines Blvd.
Pembroke Pines, FL 33024
305-987-1444

Bagel Restaurant
625 E. Atlantic Blvd.
Pompano Beach, FL 33060
305-943-2140

Sunrise Bagels
3350 N.W. 22nd Terr. #700B
Pompano Beach, FL 33069
305-979-4457

Bagel Snack
1291 S. Pompano Pkwy.
Pompano Beach, FL 33069
305-974-4564

Bagel Cafe II
4300 Kings Hwy. #205
Port Charlotte, FL 33980
813-743-6411

Bagel Haven
6650 S. Federal Hwy.
Port St. Lucie, FL 34952
407-461-8882

Bagel Cafe
2150 Tamiami Trail
Punta Gorda, FL 33948
813-625-4456

Better Bagels
7119 S Tamiami Trail
Sarasota, FL 34231
813-924-0393

Better Bagels
4804 S. Tamiami Trail
Sarasota, FL 34231
813-924-0408

Bagel Inn
1902 Bay Rd.
Sarasota, FL 34239
813-366-8988

Corey's Bagels
692 E. Eau Gallie Blvd.
Satellite Beach, FL 32937
407-777-7074

Bagel Port
13260 U.S. Hwy. 1
Sebastian, FL 32958
407-388-3438

Goody Bagels
7245 S.W. 57th Ct.
South Miami, FL 33143
305-666-4008

Goody Bakery
7222 S. Red Rd.
South Miami, FL 33143
305-666-1008

Bagel King of Springhill
2412 Commercial Way
Spring Hill, FL 34606
904-688-4444

St. Pete Bagel Company
249 Central Ave.
St. Petersburg, FL 33701
813-822-4092

St. Pete Bagel Company
6393 9th St. N
St. Petersburg, FL 33702
813-522-3377

Bagels Unlimited
5564 66th St. N
St. Petersburg, FL 33709
813-545-2234

Bagel Magic
2234 S.E. Federal Hwy.
Stuart, FL 34994
407-286-9121

Toojay's
2504 S.E. Federal Hwy.
Stuart, FL 34994
407-287-6514

Bagel Peddler's New York Deli
1410 Market St.
Tallahassee, FL 32312
904-668-2345

Julie's Bagel Joint & Deli
4299 W. Commercial Blvd.
Tamarac, FL 33319
305-739-0200

Bagel Break
6850 N. University Dr.
Tamarac, FL 33321
305-721-6030

Bagel Outlet & Delicatessen
8802 Rocky Creek Dr.
Tampa, FL 33615
813-886-9432

Bagels on 56th St.
10817 N. 56th St.
Tampa, FL 33617
813-988-9123

Tampa Bagels
10053 N. Dale Mabry Hwy.
Tampa, FL 33618
813-961-9875

A Taste of New York
1155 S. Dale Mabry Hwy.
Tampa, FL 33629
813-282-3736

Sunshine Bagel Company
1540 S. Dale Mabry Hwy.
Tampa, FL 33629
813-251-6888

Ultimate Bagel & Sandwich Shop
16019 Tampa Palms Blvd. W
Tampa, FL 33647
813-971-3028

Bagel Oasis
1811 Tamiami Trail S
Venice, FL 34293
813-493-2095

Bagel World Restaurant
4720 Okeechobee Blvd.
W. Palm Beach, FL 33417
407-686-5584

Palm Beach Kosher Market
5085 Okeechobee Blvd.
W. Palm Beach, FL 33417
407-686-2066

Toojay's
1683 Forum Plaza
West Palm Beach, FL 33401
407-697-9667

Toojay's
2911 N. Military Trail
West Palm Beach, FL 33409
407-687-4584

Bagel King Bakery-Deli Nosh
3092 Aloma Ave.
Winter Park, FL 32792
407-657-6700

GEORGIA

The Royal Bagel
1544 Piedmont Ave. NE
Atlanta, GA 30324
404-876-3512

Bagel Eatery
6631 Roswell Rd. NE #K
Atlanta, GA 30328
404-256-4411

Goldberg & Son
4383 Roswell Rd. NE
Atlanta, GA 30342
404-256-3751

Harry Barron Delicatessen
1230 Peachtree NE
Atlanta, GA 30309
404-607-6888

Bagel Palace Bakery & Deli
2869 N. Druid Hills Rd. NE
Atlanta, GA 30329
404-315-9016

Bagelicious
1255 Johnson Ferry Rd. NE
Marietta, GA 30068
404-509-9505

Gottliebs Bakery
1601 Bull St.
Savannah, GA 31401
912-355-1765

HAWAII

Sweet Overtures
Captain Cook, HI 96704
808-328-2587

Hawaiian Bagel
753 Halekauwila St.
Honolulu, HI 96813
808-523-8638

IDAHO

Bagel Bakery
606 N. 8th St.
Boise, ID 83702
208-334-6868

Pastry Perfection
3255 N. Cole Rd.
Boise, ID 83704
208-376-6303

ILLINOIS

Goodman's Bagel Bakery
1209 S. Main St.
Algonquin, IL 60102
708-658-8382

Jacob's Brothers Bagels
53 W. Jackson Blvd.
Chicago, IL 60604
312-922-2245

Jacob's Brothers Bagels
50 E. Chicago Ave.
Chicago, IL 60611
312-664-0026

Kaufman's Bagel Bakery
4411 N. Kedzie
Chicago, IL 60625
312-267-1680

Bagel Train Deli
500 W. Madison St.
Chicago, IL 60661
312-906-3939

Arnie's Bagels
1001 W. North Ave.
Chicago, IL 60635
312-944-0745

Big Apple Bagels Tree
7230 W. North Ave.
Elmwood Park, IL 60635
708-453-4646

Manhattan Bagel & Bialy
18353 S. Halsted St.
Glenwood, IL 60425
708-754-6226

Bagels & More
801 E. Roosevelt Rd.
Lombard, IL 60148
708-932-1050

Skolniks Bagel Bakery
22 E. Chicago Ave.
Naperville, IL 60540
708-355-8488

Big Apple Bagels
1220 W. Ogden Ave.
Naperville, IL 60563
708-369-4333

Bagels & More
216 Harrison St.
Oak Park, IL 60304
708-524-2424

Bagels Experience
12341 Harlem Ave.
Palos Heights, IL 60463
708-361-9993

Bagels-N-More
4700 N. University
Peoria, IL 61614
309-692-4431

Bagel Place
3600 E. State St.
Rockford, IL 61108
815-399-2522

Bagel Factory Outlet
9179 Gross Point Rd.
Skokie, IL 60077
708-674-0488

The Great American Bagel
353 W. Ogden Ave.
Westmont, IL 60559
708-963-3393

INDIANA

Brad's Bagel & Deli
1799 E. 10th
Bloomington, IN 47408
812-333-1800

Bagel King & World's Best Bagel
5447 E. 82nd St.
Castelton, IN 46250
317-842-5595

Bagel Station
5719 Saint Joe Rd.
Fort Wayne, IN 46835
219-486-7721

Bagel Fair
1300 E. 86th St.
Indianapolis, IN 46240
317-846-0950

D'Amico's Deli & Bagel
9546 Allissonville Rd.
Indianapolis, IN 46250
317-845-5463

Harlan Bakeries
7768 Zionsville Rd.
Indianapolis, IN 46268
317-875-5595

IOWA

Bruegger's Bagel Bakery
115 3rd. Ave. SE
Cedar Rapids, IA 52401
319-364-6383

Bruegger's Bagel Bakery
225 Iowa Ave.
Iowa City, IA 52240
319-354-5343

Bruegger's Bagel Bakery
715 S. Riverside Dr.
Iowa City, IA 52246
319-337-6795

Nosh Deli-Bagelry
800 1st St.
West Des Moines, IA 50265
515-255-4047

Skolniks Bagel Bakery
1551 Valley West Mall
West Des Moines, IA 50265
515-224-1111

KANSAS

Ali Baba Bakery
1025 W. 29th St.
Wichita, KS 67204
316-832-0711

Bagel & Bagel
4949 W. 119th St.
Overland Park, KS 66209
913-338-2080

KENTUCKY

Willy'z Bagel Place
902 Dupont Rd.
Louisville, KY 40207
502-897-5088

Skolniks Deli Bagelry
9980 Linn Station Rd.
Louisville, KY 40223
502-426-5673

LOUISIANA

Bagel Bayou
3474 Drusilla Ln.
Baton Rouge, LA 70809
504-928-5292

Bagel Factory
3113 N. Causeway Blvd.
Metairie, LA 70002
504-837-8707

MAINE

Mister Bagel
336 Center St.
Auburn, ME 04210
207-777-7007

The Bagel Shop
1 Main St.
Bangor, ME 04401
207-947-1654

Go Bagel Shop
1111 Middle
Portland, ME 04101
207-879-1962

Mister Bagel
601 Forest Ave.
Portland, ME 04106
207-775-0718

Mister Bagel
100 Waterman Dr.
South Portland, ME 04106
207-767-4756

MARYLAND

Bagel Cafe
Harborplace
Baltimore, MD 21202
410-547-0210

Bagel Shop
105 E. Baltimore St.
Baltimore, MD 21202
410-576-1191

Greg's Bagels
Belvedere Square
Baltimore, MD 21212
410-323-9463

Baltimore Bagel
1032 Light St.
Baltimore, MD 21230
410-426-1676

**Baltimore Bagel &
Delivery Co.**
4215 Fitch Ave.
Baltimore, MD 21236
410-665-9611

Bagel Master
12012 Old Baltimore Pike
Beltsville, MD 20705
301-937-2100

Bethesda Bagel
4819 Bethesda Ave.
Bethesda, MD 20814
301-652-8990

Chesapeake Bagel Bakery
7700 Norfolk Ave.
Bethesda, MD 20814
301-654-5744

Cockeysville Bagel Bakery
120 Cranbrook Rd.
Cockeysville, MD 21030
410-667-4007

Bagel Shoppe of Columbia
10451 Twin Rivers Rd.
Columbia, MD 21044
410-740-0024

Bagels 'N More
6955 Oakland Mills Rd.
Columbia, MD 21045
410-290-9387

Bagel Shoppe
8630 Guilford Rd.
Columbia, MD 21046
410-381-1730

Beegals Bagels
701 Russell Ave.
Gaithersburg, MD 20877
301-948-8915

Chesapeake Bagel Bakery
7423 Greenbelt Rd.
Greenbelt, MD 20770
301-474-1114

New York Bagel & Deli
11805 Coastal Hwy.
Ocean City, MD 21842
410-524-7645

Bagel Shoppe
11406 Reisterstown Rd.
Owings Mills, MD 21117
410-356-7200

Bagel Shoppe
10300 Mill Run Circle
Owings Mills, MD 21117
410-363-7012

Bagel Shoppe
506 Reisterstown Rd.
Pikesville, MD 21208
410-484-8202

Bagel Shoppe
8015 Liberty Rd.
Randallstown, MD 21133
410-922-8844

Bagel City
12119 Rockville Pike
Rockville, MD 20852
301-231-8080

Chesapeake Bagel Bakery
865 Rockville Pike #D
Rockville, MD 20852
301-738-3788

Hofberg's
5240 Randolph Rd.
Rockville, MD 20852
301-770-0777

Skolniks
White Flint Mall
Rockville, MD 20852
301-984-5760

The Bagelry
36 Vital Way
Silver Spring, MD 20904
301-384-2322

Parkway Deli
8317 Grubb Rd.
Silver Spring, MD 20910
301-587-1427

Not Just Bagels
White Marsh Mall
White Marsh, MD 21162
410-931-9085

MASSACHUSETTS

Bruegger's Bagel Bakery
32 Bromfield St.
Boston, MA 02108
617-357-5577

Bruegger's Bagel Bakery
279 Massachusetts Ave.
Boston, MA 02115
617-536-6003

Bruegger's Bagel Bakery
636 Beacon St.
Boston, MA 02215
617-262-7939

Ultimate Bagel Company
335 Newbury St.
Boston, MA 02115
617-247-1010

Zade's Bagel Express
100 Massachusetts Ave.
Boston, MA 02141
617-252-9033

Eagerman's Bakery
415 Harvard St.
Brookline, MA 02124
617-566-8771

Bruegger's Bagel Bakery
83 Mt. Auburn St.
Cambridge, MA 02138
617-661-4664

Bagel Land
635 Washington St.
Canton, MA 02021
617-828-1769

Katz Bagel Bakery
139 Park
Chelsea, MA 02150
617-884-9738

Bagel Place of College Park
7423 Baltimore Blvd.
College Park, MA 20740
301-779-3900

New York Bagel Company
239 State Rd.
Dartmouth, MA 02714
508-990-3350

New York Bagel Company
1706 President Ave.
Fall River, MA 02720
508-677-4767

Bagels Bagels Bagels
1243 Worcester Rd.
Framingham, MA 01701
508-872-7251

Bagel Land of Cape Cod
88 North St.
Hyannis, MA 02601
508-790-0089

Kimmel's Bagel Shop
786 Williams St.
Longmeadow, MA 01106
413-567-3304

Bagel Bar
191 Pleasant
Marblehead, MA 01945
617-639-0301

Eagerman's Bakery
810 Worcester
Natick, MA 01760
617-235-1092

Bruegger's Bagel Bakery
2050 Commonwealth Ave.
Newton, MA 02166
617-964-9508

Rosenfeld Bagel Company
1280 Centre St.
Newton, MA 02159
617-527-8080

Ultimate Bagel
118 Needham St.
Newton, MA 02164
617-964-8990

Bagel Deli
96 Main St.
Northampton, MA 01060
413-586-3687

Zappy's Bagel Bakery
937 N. Main
Randolph, MA 02368
617-963-9837

Zade's Bagel Shop
120 Broadway
Saugus, MA 01906
617-233-3080

Bruegger's Bagel Bakery
1441 Main St.
Springfield, MA 01103
413-788-8701

Bagel Baker
621 Boston Post Rd.
Sudbury, MA 01776
508-443-7033

Bruegger's Bagel Bakery
251 Washington St.
Wellesley, MA 02181
617-235-8466

Arthur's Bagels & Friends
119 June St.
Worcester, MA 01602
508-757-3835

MICHIGAN

Bagel Factory
1306 S. University Ave.
Ann Arbor, MI 48104
313-663-3345

Barry's Bagel Place
2517 Jackson Rd.
Ann Arbor, MI 48103
313-662-2435

Detroit Bagel Factories
1900 S. Woodward Ave.
Bloomfield Hills, MI 48302
313-641-9188

Bagel King
26424 Ford Rd.
Dearborn Heights, MI 48127
313-563-6009

Bagel-Fragel Deli
521 E. Grand River Ave.
East Lansing, MI 48823
517-332-0300

Broadway Bagel & Deli
24225 Orchard Lake Rd.
Farmington Hills, MI 48336
313-471-5404

New York Bagel
23316 Woodward Ave.
Ferndale, MI 48220
313-548-2580

Bagel-Haul Deli
1641 Haslett Rd.
Haslett, MI 48840
517-339-3634

Bagel Restaurant & Deli
13928 Woodward
Highland Park, MI 48203
313-867-0003

Broadway Bagel
1700 John Papalas Dr.
Lincoln Park, MI 48146
313-386-6338

New York Bagel
25246 Greenfield Rd.
Oak Park, MI 48237
313-967-3919

Bagel Factory Of Southfield
24551 W. 12 Mile Rd.
Southfield, MI 48034
313-352-5695

New York Bagel Baking Co.
19731 W. 12 Mile Rd.
Southfield, MI 48076
313-559-6591

Grand Traverse Bagel Factory
1327 S. Airport Rd.
Traverse City, MI 49684
616-947-0337

Hershel's Deli & Hot Bakery
585 W. Big Beaver Rd.
Troy, MI 48084
313-524-4770

New York Bagel
6927 Orchard Lake Rd.
West Bloomfield, MI 48322
313-851-9210

MINNESOTA

Bruegger's Bagel Bakery
44th & France Ave. S
Edina, MN 55422
612-927-9446

Bruegger's Bagel Bakery
1100 Nicollet Mall
Minneapolis, MN 55403
612-338-3142

Bruegger's Bagel Bakery
1920 Portland Ave.
Minneapolis, MN 55414
612-871-3948

Bruegger's Bagel Bakery
1500 W. Lake St.
Minneapolis, MN 55408
612-823-2756

Bruegger's Bagel Bakery
800 Washington Ave. SE
Minneapolis, MN 55414
612-378-2145

Bruegger's Bagel Bakery
319 14th Ave. SE
Minneapolis, MN 55414
612-623-9522

Bruegger's Bagel Bakery
3558 Winnetka Ave. N
New Hope, MN 55427
612-545-6783

New York Bakery & Bagels
8128 Minnetonka Blvd.
St. Louis Park, MN 55426
612-933-3535

Bruegger's Bagel Bakery
796 Grand Ave.
St. Paul, MN 55105
612-221-1909

Bruegger's Bagel Bakery
2136 Ford Pkwy.
St. Paul, MN 55116
612-699-8011

Twin City Bagel
149 Thompson Ave. E
West St. Paul, MN 55118
612-451-5977

MISSOURI

Bagel and Bagel
6322 Brookside Plaza
Kansas City, MO 64113
816-333-2080

The Bagel Factory
11256 Olive St.
St. Louis, MO 63141
314-432-3383

Petrofsky's Bagels
7649 Delmar Blvd.
St. Louis, MO 63130
314-432-5101

New York Bakery & Bagelry
8625 Olive St.
St. Louis, MO 63130
314-993-9440

MONTANA

Donut Hole
1500 Broadwater Ave.
Billings, MT 59102
406-652-6565

Donut Hole
926 Main St.
Billings, MT 59105
406-259-1400

Bozeman Bagelworks
708 W. Main
Bozeman, MT 59715
406-585-1727

NEBRASKA

Hole Works
1227 R St.
Lincoln, NE 68508
402-435-6931

Mettler Family Bakery
821 S. 11th St.
Lincoln, NE 68508
402-474-5644

Bagel Bin Inc.
1215 S. 119th Ct.
Omaha, NE 68144
402-334-2744

NEVADA

Bagelmania
855 E. Twain Ave.
Las Vegas, NV 89109
702-369-3322

Bagel Oasis
9134 W. Sahara
Las Vegas, NV 89117
702-363-0811

Jamie's Restaurant
4725 S. Maryland Pkwy.
Las Vegas, NV 89119
702-736-8122

Bagel Deli
2600 S. Virginia St.
Reno, NV 89502
702-825-8866

NEW HAMPSHIRE

Bagels & Bites
270 Loudon Rd.
Concord, NH 03301
603-228-0181

Keen Bagel Works
120 Main St.
Keene, NH 03431
603-357-7751

The Bagel Boys Inc.
545 Daniel Webster Hwy.
Manchester, NH 03103
603-623-4436

Bagel Connection
101 D J Sq.
Merrimack, NH 03054
603-881-9635

The Bagel Alley
1 Eldridge St.
Nashua, NH 03060
603-882-9343

The Bagelry
19 Market St.
Portsmouth, NH 03801
603-431-5853

NEW JERSEY

Eli's Hot Bagels
Hwy. 34
Aberdeen Township, NJ 07747
908-566-4523

Bagel Gourmet
162 S. New York Rd.
Absecon, NJ 08201
609-748-1600

Bagel King
1624 St. George Ave.
Avenel, NJ 07001
908-382-0315

Randy's Hot Bagel Bakery
Hwy. 9
Barnegat, NJ 08005
609-698-0616

Country Bagel & Deli
787 Rte. 9
Bayville, NJ 08721
908-269-5551

Bagel Bop
670 Amwell Mall
Belle Mead, NJ 08502
908-359-7929

Freedman's Bakery
803 Main St.
Belmar, NJ 07719
908-681-2334

J C S Bagels
55 N. Washington Ave.
Bergenfield, NJ 07626
201-385-6642

Cambridge Bagel Factory
648 Bloomfield Ave.
Bloomfield, NJ 07003
201-743-5683

Bagelsmith Deli
159 Hwy. 202
Branchburg, NJ 08876
908-369-8779

Bagel & Lox
18 Brick Plaza
Brick, NJ 08723
908-477-9020

Julie's Bagel Nook
2526 Hooper
Brick, NJ 08723
908-920-4546

Bagel Factory
1905 Rte. 88
Brick, NJ 08724
908-840-7511

Bagelsmith Deli
1330 Prince Rogers Ave.
Bridgewater, NJ 08807
908-725-7040

J & J's Bakery
Hwy. 46
Budd Lake, NJ 07828
201-691-1714

Bagels N' Stuff
313 High St.
Burlington, NJ 08016
609-386-0448

Bagel Inn
897 Bloomfield Ave.
Caldwell, NJ 07006
201-227-9871

Bagelsmith
Rte. 513-Neighbors Plaza
Califon, NJ 07830
908-832-7940

Bagel By The Bay
3704 Bayshore Rd.
Cape May, NJ 08204
609-886-0966

Bodacious Bagels Restaurant
727 Beach Dr.
Cape May, NJ 08204
609-884-3031

Cheese & Bagel Shop
641 Shunpike Rd.
Chatham, NJ 07878
201-822-2114

Skolniks Bagel Bakery
Cherry Hill Mall
Cherry Hill, NJ 08002
609-662-2122

Bagel Place
Kings Highway & Chapel Ave.
Cherry Hill, NJ 08034
609-667-3944

Cinnaminson Bagle Shop
Hwy. 130 & Church Rd.
Cinnaminson, NJ 08077
609-829-9093

Clark Bagels
1115 Raritan Rd.
Clark, NJ 07066
908-382-2435

Hot Bagels
1460 Blackwood Clementon Rd.
Clementon, NJ 08021
609-784-4037

Cliffside Park Bagels
711 Anderson Ave.
Cliffside Park, NJ 07010
201-945-4808

Clifton Bagel Bakery
391 Piaget Ave.
Clifton, NJ 07011
201-478-4650

Main Avenue Bagel
1119 Main Ave.
Clifton, NJ 07011
201-779-4675

Bagel Chateau
72 Market St.
Clifton, NJ 07012
201-365-9779

Bagel King II
754 Clifton Ave.
Clifton, NJ 07013
201-470-8140

Plaza Bagel & Deli
850 Van Houten Ave.
Clifton, NJ 07013
201-777-2094

Bagelsmith Food Store
Hwy. 31 S
Clinton, NJ 08809
908-735-6634

Bagel Palace
258 Closter Dock Rd.
Closter, NJ 07624
201-768-2417

Bakery & Bagelry
67 Closter Plaza
Closter, NJ 07624
201-767-1441

Colonia Hot Bagels
560 Inman Ave.
Colonia, NJ 07067
908-574-3522

Bagel America
123 N. Union Ave.
Cranford, NJ 07016
908-276-9598

Cresskill Hot Bagels
23 Union Ave.
Cresskill, NJ 07626
201-569-3909

Deal Bagel
296 Norwood Ave.
Deal, NJ 07723
908-517-8500

Denville Bagel & Deli
109 E. Main St.
Denville, NJ 07834
201-586-3441

Bagel Builders
Deptford Mall
Deptford, NJ 08096
609-853-0040

Goldie Lox Bagels
76 Washington Ave.
Dumont, NJ 07628
201-385-0130

Manhattan Bagel Company
390 North Ave.
Dunellen, NJ 08812
908-968-9172

Bagel Mania
434 Ridgedale Rd.
East Hanover, NJ 07936
201-884-0602

Bagel Boys
613 Hope Rd.
Eatontown, NJ 07724
908-389-3344

Bagel Bazaar
95 Hgwy. 27
Edison, NJ 08820
908-494-9677

Metro Edison Bagel Bakery
1655 Oak Tree Rd.
Edison, NJ 08820
908-548-8857

Designer Bagels
2849 Woodbridge Ave.
Edison, NJ 08837
908-603-0083

Elmora Bagel Bakery
183 Elmora Ave.
Elizabeth, NJ 07202
908-289-2985

Bagel Chateau
100 Broadway
Elmwood Park, NJ 07407
201-796-7709

Bagel King
71 Hwy. 46
Elmwood Park, NJ 07407
201-791-8522

Hot Bagels
185 Kinderkamack Rd.
Emerson, NJ 07630
201-261-2947

Englewood Bagel
54 E. Palisade Ave.
Englewood, NJ 07631
201-567-4500

Bagel World
300 Hwy. 9
Englishtown, NJ 07726
908-536-8144

Englishtown Bagels
Old Bridge-Englishtown Rd.
Englishtown, NJ 07726
908-446-2280

Hot Bagels
6-07 Saddle River Rd.
Fair Lawn, NJ 07410
201-796-9625

River Road Hot Bagels
13-38 River Rd.
Fair Lawn, NJ 07410
201-791-5646

We Ain't Just Bagels
39-26 Broadway
Fair Lawn, NJ 07410
201-791-7755

Bagelsmith Restaurant
31 Main St.
Flemington, NJ 08822
908-782-4800

Bagels 4-U
187 Columbia Turnpike
Florham Park, NJ 07932
201-966-1634

Bagel Connection & Restaurant
403 N. Main
Forked River, NJ 08731
609-971-7747

Fort Lee Bagels
247 Main St.
Fort Lee, NJ 07024
201-592-9823

Sid's Hot Bagels
2040 Lemoine Ave.
Fort Lee, NJ 07024
201-947-8150

Hot Bagel Stop
Rte. 23
Franklin, NJ 07416
201-827-7711

Bagel Express
3029 Hwy. 27
Franklin, NJ 08823
908-297-4453

Bagels By Michael
Freehold Shopping Center
Freehold, NJ 07728
908-308-3282

Hot Bagel Shop
347 W. Main St.
Freehold, NJ 07728
908-431-5144

Eli's Hot Bagels
Hwy. 9
Freehold, NJ 07728
908-780-3536

New York Hot Bagels
3333 Hwy. 9
North Freehold, NJ 07728
908-577-7951

Bagel Hop
503 Midland Ave.
Garfield, NJ 07026
201-340-8001

Don's Bagels
2 Doubletree Shopping Center
Glassboro, NJ 08028
609-582-4455

Bagel Gourmet
235 Rock Rd.
Glen Rock, NJ 07452
201-652-9822

Bakery & Bagelry
918 Prospect Rd.
Glen Rock, NJ 07452
201-445-2595

Bagelsmith Food Store
285 Hwy. 22
Green Brook, NJ 08812
908-752-5566

Big Girl Bagels
134 Main St.
Hackensack, NJ 07601
201-487-4470

Classic Bagel
116 Anderson St.
Hackensack, NJ 07601
201-487-2468

Main Street Bagel & Deli
186 Main St.
Hackensack, NJ 07601
201-489-3494

Harper's Bagel & Bake Shop
265 Main St.
Hackettstown, NJ 07840
908-852-8585

Bagelsmith Foodstores
Van Sycles Rd.
Hampton, NJ 08827
908-730-8600

Bagelsmith Foodstores
Rte. 78
Hampton, NJ 08827
908-735-9866

Not Just Bagels
200 Boulevard
Hasbrouck Heights, NJ 07604
201-288-2555

Bagel Odyssey
1185 Ringwood Ave.
Haskell, NJ 07420
201-835-0155

Manhattan Bagel
3250 Highway 35 N
Hazlet, NJ 07730
908-888-7717

Bagel Dish
70 Raritan Ave.
Highland Park, NJ 08904
908-828-3474

Bagel Town
Hwy. 130
Hightstown, NJ 08520
609-448-4675

Twin Rivers Bagel
101-2 Abbington Dr.
Hightstown, NJ 08520
609-443-8330

Ronnie's Hillside Hot Bagels
118 Broadway
Hillside, NJ 07642
201-664-4543

Hoboken Bagels
634 Washington St.
Hoboken, NJ 07030
201-798-9640

J P's Bagel Express
64 Newark St.
Hoboken, NJ 07030
201-963-5522

Uptown Bagel & Deli
112 14th St.
Hoboken, NJ 07030
201-656-3450

Zaro's Home Bakery
Holmdel Plaza
Holmdel, NJ 07733
908-264-4406

Bagel Country
4014 Hwy. 9
Howell, NJ 07731
908-363-1092

Kristina's Bakery
Ramtown Plaza
Howell, NJ 07731
908-840-8869

T R Bagels
100 Applegrath Rd.
Jamesburg, NJ 08831
908-655-9636

Central Avenue Bagels
293 Central Ave.
Jersey City, NJ 07307
201-798-9311

I Love Bagels
700 Kenilworth Blvd.
Kenilworth, NJ 07033
908-245-3838

Hot Bagels of Cliffwood
198 Hwy. 35 N
Keyport, NJ 07735
908-583-0502

Howard's Bagel Bakery
82 N. Beverwyck Rd.
Lake Hiawatha, NJ 07034
201-299-0116

Bagel America
2128 Hwy. 70
Lakehurst, NJ 08733
908-657-2015

Bagel Delight
1203 Airport Rd.
Lakewood, NJ 08701
908-905-7780

Bagel Nosh
210 Clifton Ave.
Lakewood, NJ 08701
908-363-1115

Bagelsmith Foodstores
Hwy. 22
Lebanon, NJ 08833
908-236-9808

Famous Fort Lee Bagels
332 Broad Ave.
Leonia, NJ 07605
201-592-1998

Whatta Bagel
60 Beaverbrook Rd.
Lincoln Park, NJ 07035
201-305-1101

Bagels Unlimited
163 Main St.
Little Falls, NJ 07424
201-785-2211

T & L Bagels Plus
315 Main St.
Little Ferry, NJ 07643
201-641-8030

Bagel Shop
Livingston Mall
Livingston, NJ 07039
201-533-9438

Bagels Of Livingston
37 E. Northfield Rd.
Livingston, NJ 07039
201-994-1915

Super Duper Bagels
498 S. Livingston Ave.
Livingston, NJ 07039
201-533-1703

Bib's Premium Bagels
79 Main St.
Lodi, NJ 07644
201-614-0656

Essex Bagels
330 Essex St.
Lodi, NJ 07644
201-368-8224

Bonforte Upper Crust Deli
444 Ocean Blvd.
Long Branch, NJ 07740
908-571-0066

Plaza Deli & Bagel Shop
27 Madison Plaza
Madison, NJ 07940
201-966-1117

Bagel Chateau of Maplewood
180 Maplewood Ave.
Maplewood, NJ 07040
201-762-1707

Bagel Time Deli
Hwy. 9 & Union Hill Rd.
Marlboro, NJ 07746
908-536-4616

Bagel Place Too
Plaza 70 E
Marlton, NJ 08053
609-983-5151

Bagels And
230 N. Maple Ave.
Marlton, NJ 08053
609-983-6165

Bakin Bagels
56 W. Pleasant Ave.
Maywood, NJ 07607
201-843-9480

New York Bagels
Hwy. 70 & Jennings Rd.
Medford, NJ 08055
609-654-4686

Bagel Street
110 Flock Rd.
Mercerville, NJ 08619
609-584-1414

Bagel Supreme
726 Union Ave.
Middlesex, NJ 08846
908-356-2820

Bagel Corner
1109 Hwy. 35
Middletown, NJ 07748
908-671-7875

Bagelsmith Restaurants
Rte. 2
Milford, NJ 08848
908-996-9823

Bagel Chateau
321 Millburn Ave.
Millburn, NJ 07041
201-376-9691

Bagel Express
100 Ryders Ln.
Milltown, NJ 08850
908-745-2177

Mine Hill Bagel & Deli
231 Hwy. 46
Mine Hill, NJ 07801
201-328-4800

The Bagelrie
4095 Hwy. 1
Monmouth Junction, NJ 08852
908-329-6969

Bagel Shop
24 Chestnut Ridge Rd.
Montvale, NJ 07645
201-391-9756

B & M Hot Bagels
Hwy. 38
Mt. Holly, NJ 08060
609-267-0557

New York Bagels
3747 Church Rd.
Mt. Laurel, NJ 08054
609-722-8999

Abel's Bagels
45 Easton Ave.
New Brunswick, NJ 08901
908-214-8384

T R Bagel Inc.
1 Penn Plaza
New Brunswick, NJ 08901
908-828-3545

Brooklyn Bagel Masters
32 Commerce Ct.
Newark, NJ 07102
201-504-9111

Spring Street Bagels
129 Spring St.
Newton, NJ 07860
201-579-1690

Bagel Factory
293 Ridge Rd.
North Arlington, NJ 07031
201-997-0660

Twin Bagels
440 Ridge Rd.
North Arlington, NJ 07031
201-991-2697

Bagel Stop
1898 Hwy. 130
North Brunswick, NJ 08902
908-422-8700

Bagel Chef
510 Livingston St.
Norwood, NJ 07648
201-767-3596

Bagel Time
226 Franklin Ave.
Nutley, NJ 07110
201-661-4455

Hot Bagel Bakery
65 Monmouth Rd.
Oakhurst, NJ 07755
908-870-6262

Oakland Bagel & Pastry
347 Ramapo Valley Rd.
Oakland, NJ 07436
201-405-1222

Chompie's Bagel Noshery
885 W. Park Ave.
Ocean, NJ 07712
908-493-8885

Bagel Dip'n Deli
40114 West Ave.
Ocean City, NJ 08226
609-398-3354

Golden Bagels
7 Fairway Ln.
Old Bridge, NJ 08857
908-721-7082

Goldberg's Famous Bagels
390 Kinderkamack Rd.
Oradell, NJ 07649
201-265-6717

Bagel Emporium
67 E. Ridgewood Ave.
Paramus, NJ 07652
201-262-9778

Goldberg's Famous Bagels
183 Kinderkamack Rd.
Park Ridge, NJ 07656
201-573-8845

Bagel Barn
134 Baldwin Rd.
Parsippany, NJ 07054
201-335-1217

Bagels of Parsippany
294 U.S. Hwy. 46
Parsippany, NJ 07054
201-575-4380

Plaza Bagel Shop
748 U.S. Hwy. 46
Parsippany, NJ 07054
201-263-9249

Passaic Park Bagel Bakery
201 Main Ave.
Passaic, NJ 07055
201-614-9475

Bagel Feast
429 Jelsma
Paterson, NJ 07501
201-345-6360

Deli On A Bagel
1314 Centennial Ave.
Piscataway, NJ 08854
908-562-0777

Manhattan Bagel
1665 Stelton Rd.
Piscataway, NJ 08854
908-985-2511

Bagel Stop II
1109 South Ave.
Plainfield, NJ 07062
908-754-7777

Skolniks
Hamilton Mall
Pleasantville, NJ 08232
609-272-1382

K C's Bagel Express
443 Hwy. 23
Pompton Plains, NJ 07444
201-835-0438

D'Orsi Bakery
479 Port Reading Ave.
Port Reading , NJ 07064
908-634-7994

Princeton Bakery
Princeton Shopping Center
Princeton, NJ 08540
609-924-9617

Abel Bagel
32 Witherspoon Ln.
Princeton, NJ 08542
609-921-9745

Bagelicious
2259 Bridge Ave.
Pt. Pleasant Beach, NJ 08742
908-892-9265

Corner Bagelry
600 Arnold Ave.
Pt. Pleasant Beach, NJ 08742
908-295-5484

Bagel Depot
37 W. Cherry St.
Rahway, NJ 07065
908-815-1499

Bagel Depot
51 E. Main St.
Ramsey, NJ 07446
201-327-9312

Bagel Express
486 Hwy 10 N
Randolph, NJ 07869
201-328-4499

Bagel Inn
Rte. 10
Randolph, NJ 07869
201-328-9234

Bagel Oven
72 Monmouth St.
Red Bank, NJ 07701
908-842-1141

Bagel Station
168 Monmouth St.
Red Bank, NJ 07701
908-842-0002

Ridgefield Park Bagels
187 Main St.
Ridgefield Park, NJ 07660
201-440-9860

All My Bagels
49 E. Ridgewood Ave.
Ridgewood, NJ 07450
201-444-3305

Bagelicious
19 N. Broad St.
Ridgewood, NJ 07450
201-652-9421

Ringwood Bagels
55 Skyline Dr.
Ringwood, NJ 07456
201-962-9834

Goldberg's Bagels
216 Riverdale Rd.
Riverdale, NJ 07675
201-358-9116

Cherry Hill Bakery & Bagelry
1059 Main St.
River Edge, NJ 07661
201-487-0660

River Edge Bagels & Bakery
645 Kinderkamack Rd.
River Edge, NJ 07661
201-262-6370

Bagelworks
15 Park Ave.
Rutherford, NJ 07070
201-933-0211

Bagels & Beyond
460 Market St.
Saddle Brook, NJ 07662
201-845-6662

Manhattan Bagel
881 Main
Sayreville, NJ 08872
908-525-0696

Max's Hot Bagels
499 Ernston Rd.
Sayreville, NJ 08872
908-721-3222

Wall To Wall Bagels
2510 Rte. 35
Sea Girt, NJ 08750
908-449-4010

Bagel Buffet
127 Plaza Centre
Secaucus, NJ 07094
201-863-1710

Bagels Plus
Harmon Meadows Pkwy.
Secaucus, NJ 07094
201-330-0744

Bagel Eddi's
18th & Long Beach Blvd.
Ship Bottom, NJ 08008
609-494-4761

Everything On A Bagel
20 S. White Horse Pike
Somerdale, NJ 08083
609-346-1114

Bagel Express
1217 Hwy. 27
Somerset, NJ 08873
908-545-8621

Bagel Peddler
1075 Easton Ave.
Somerset, NJ 08873
908-246-9045

Bagel Peddler
53 W. Main St.
Somerville, NJ 08876
908-526-9733

Bagel Stop
23 S. Plainfield Ave.
South Plainfield, NJ 07080
908-561-5808

Chubbs Bagel Restaurant
4949 Stelton Rd.
South Plainfield, NJ 07080
908-757-8877

Bagel Depot
41 Ferry St.
South River, NJ 08882
908-613-9112

Wanna Bagel & Bake Shop II
43 Theatre Center
Sparta, NJ 07871
201-729-5099

Bagel Shoppe
365 Spotswood Englishtown Rd.
Spotswood, NJ 08884
908-251-8118

Manhattan Bagel Company
100 Summerhill Rd.
Spotswood, NJ 08884
908-251-8857

Benny's Five Bagels
101 Hwy. 71
Spring Lake, NJ 07762
908-449-3834

Bagels Supreme
252 Mountain Ave.
Springfield, NJ 07081
201-376-9381

Bagel Break
Roxbury Mall
Succaunna, NJ 07876
201-927-6311

Bagel Palace
402 Cedar Ln.
Teaneck, NJ 07666
201-836-4660

Hot Bagels
513 Cedar Ln.
Teaneck, NJ 07666
201-836-9705

Tenafly Hot Bagels
35 Washington Ave.
Tenafly, NJ 07670
201-567-2935

Bagels Plus
915 Fischer Blvd.
Toms River, NJ 08753
908-929-4369

Bagels Plus
1 Washington St.
Toms River, NJ 08753
908-505-8803

Silverton Bagels
1831 Hooper Ave.
Toms River, NJ 08753
908-255-4450

Toms River Bagels
Rte. 37 E
Toms River, NJ 08753
908-341-8056

Brooklyn Bagels
345 Union Blvd.
Totowa, NJ 07512
201-595-1633

Paulie's Bagel Bakery Cafe
440 Main Rd.
Towaco, NJ 07082
201-316-6900

Kramer's Bagels Plus
1700 Nottingham Way
Trenton, NJ 08619
609-586-3113

Bagel Junction
171 Mercer Mall
Trenton, NJ 08648
609-452-9876

Bagel Junction
1100 Hwy. 33
Trenton, NJ 08690
609-890-9617

Hot Bagels & More
Town Center
Turnersville, NJ 08012
609-228-2992

Bagel Builder
2445 Springfield Ave.
Union, NJ 07083
908-686-1911

5 Points Bagels & Deli
1350 Galloping Hill Rd.
Union, NJ 07083
908-688-0709

Lox Stock & Bagels
6433 Ventnor Ave.
Ventnor City, NJ 08406
609-822-8621

Bagelwich Bagel Bakery
652 Bloomfield Ave.
Verona, NJ 07044
201-857-9408

Bagel Factory
219 S. Delsea Dr.
Vineland, NJ 08360
609-692-6685

Buddy's Bagels
484 N. Brewster Rd.
Vineland, NJ 08360
609-692-3555

Bagel Bin
3 Cooper Plaza
Voorhees, NJ 08043
609-346-4337

Merlin's Hot Bagels
Paddock Plaza
W. Long Branch, NJ 07764
908-544-0330

Bagels And
24-A W. Prospect
Waldwick, NJ 07463
201-652-9746

Main Bagels
45 Main Ave.
Wallington, NJ 07057
201-365-2080

Bagelsmith
Stirling Rd.
Warren, NJ 07059
908-757-1555

Bagel Boys
1055 Hamburg Pike
Wayne, NJ 07470
201-696-9833

Sam's Bagel & Deli
Plaza Square Shopping Center
Wayne, NJ 07470
201-790-0135

Willowbrook Bagels
1408 Willowbrook Mall
Wayne, NJ 07470
201-785-9767

Boogie Woogie Bagel Boys
1200 Harbor Blvd.
Weehawken, NJ 07087
201-863-4666

Bagel Place of Berlin
Highway 73 & Walker Ave.
West Berlin, NJ 08091
609-768-7766

Bagels 4 U of West Caldwell
673 Bloomfield Ave.
West Caldwell, NJ 07006
201-228-6244

Wanna Bagel & Bake Shop
1614 Union Valley Rd.
West Milford, NJ 07480
201-728-3630

Bergenline Bagels
6512 Bergenline Ave.
West New York, NJ 07093
201-868-9528

Bagel Box
642 Eagle Rock Ave.
West Orange, NJ 07052
201-731-4985

Better On A Bagel
250 Browertown Rd.
West Paterson, NJ 07424
201-256-0106

Bagel Chateau
123 Quimby St.
Westfield, NJ 07090
908-232-1921

Goldberg's Famous Bagels
425 Broadway
Westwood, NJ 07675
201-666-9896

Bagelsmith Food Stores
Hwy. 22
White House Station, NJ 08889
908-534-9992

Wyckoff Bagels
636 Wyckoff Ave.
Wyckoff, NJ 07481
201-891-6003

NEW MEXICO

New York House Of Bagels
1605 Juan Tabo Blvd. NE
Albuquerque, NM 87112
505-275-9390

Beckers Delicatessen
403 Guadaloupe
Sante Fe, NM 87501
505-988-2423

NEW YORK

Bruegger's Bagel Bakery
Stuyvesant Plaza
Albany, NY 12203
518-482-3579

Bialys Bagels & Butter
Colonie Plaza
Albany, NY 12205
518-452-2607

Bruegger's Bagel Bakery
98 Wolf Rd.
Albany, NY 12205
518-438-5014

Bagel Bite
Westgate Shopping Center
Albany, NY 12206
518-489-7202

Bruegger's Bagel Bakery
29 N. Pearl St.
Albany, NY 12207
518-463-4961

Bagel Baron
285 New Scotland Ave.
Albany, NY 12208
518-482-9264

Bruegger's Bagel Bakery
1116 Madison Ave.
Albany, NY 12208
518-489-2236

B. A. Gels Limited
189 Lark St.
Albany, NY 12210
518-463-0884

Bruegger's Bagel Bakery
4 Central Ave.
Albany, NY 12210
518-426-8373

Bagel & Bialys
1152 Willis Ave.
Albertson, NY 11507
516-621-9520

Bagel Brothers Bakery & Deli
3073 Sheridan Dr.
Amherst, NY 14226
716-837-8885

Family Bagel
782 Merrick Rd.
Baldwin, NY 11510
516-868-1980

Grand Bagels
1845 Grand Ave.
Baldwin, NY 11510
516-378-4410

Bagel Boss East
555 Montauk Hwy.
Bay Shore, NY 11706
516-665-9820

Best Bagels of Bayport
871 Montauk Hwy.
Bayport, NY 11705
516-472-6198

Bagel Club
20521 35th Ave.
Bayside, NY 11361
718-423-6106

Hot Bagels & Bake
4007 Bell Blvd.
Bayside, NY 11361
718-229-6371

Bagel Garden
442 Wantagh Ave.
Bethpage, NY 11714
516-931-8428

Binghamton Bagels
125 Robinson St.
Binghamton, NY 13904
607-724-6815

B & B Hot Bagels
4641 Sunrise Hwy.
Bohemia, NY 11716
516-563-1959

Bagel Lovers
4788 Sunrise Hwy.
Bohemia, NY 11716
516-563-8907

Little Shop of Bagels
1093 Smithtown Ave.
Bohemia, NY 11716
516-563-3535

Rogers Family Bagel
1750 Brentwood Rd.
Brentwood, NY 11717
516-435-8497

Hole in One Bagel
100 Main St.
Brewster, NY 10509
914-279-8978

Ingerson's Pastry Shop
42 Main St.
Brockport, NY 14420
716-637-0490

Mister Bagel of Broadway
5672 Broadway
Bronx, NY 10463
212-549-0408

Jerry's Bagel
3405 Jerome Ave.
Bronx, NY 10467
212-515-7111

Bagel Cafe
2214 Bartow Ave.
Bronx, NY 10475
212-320-9011

Heavenly Bagel
80 Court
Brooklyn, NY 11201
718-858-3600

Dale's Bagels
6201 18th Ave.
Brooklyn, NY 11204
718-232-0132

Bagelicious
6424 20th Ave.
Brooklyn, NY 11204
718-256-5800

Mezonos Bagels
5721 16th Ave.
Brooklyn, NY 11204
718-853-1031

What's A Bagel
11124 Flatlands Ave.
Brooklyn, NY 11207
718-257-4765

Bagel Emporium
8614 4th Ave.
Brooklyn, NY 11209
718-745-8686

Bagelicious Bagel & Deli
7622 3rd Ave.
Brooklyn, NY 11209
718-921-0505

D V A Bagels
7017 3rd Ave.
Brooklyn, NY 11209
718-748-2660

Fifth Avenue Bagel Company
7416 5th Ave.
Brooklyn, NY 11209
718-238-0075

Shore Road Bagel & Deli
9401 5th Ave.
Brooklyn, NY 11209
718-745-1108

Wanna Bagel
8905 3rd Ave.
Brooklyn, NY 11209
718-921-2600

Buttercup Bagel
754 Metropolitan Ave.
Brooklyn, NY 11211
718-782-5856

Bagel Shop
7722 18th Ave.
Brooklyn, NY 11214
718-331-4911

Tasty Bagels
1705 86th St.
Brooklyn, NY 11214
718-236-1389

Tom Kit Bagels
2472 86th St.
Brooklyn, NY 11214
718-372-6296

Uncle Bobby's Bagels
1983 86th St.
Brooklyn, NY 11214
718-373-1523

Bagel Hole
400 7th Ave.
Brooklyn, NY 11215
718-788-4014

Terrace Bagels Inc.
224 Prospect Park W
Brooklyn, NY 11215
718-768-3943

Bagel Express
120 Flatbush Ave.
Brooklyn, NY 11217
718-875-7777

Bagelicious
18 Nevins St.
Brooklyn, NY 11217
718-875-5814

Bagels N Stuff
1240 Prospect Ave.
Brooklyn, NY 11218
718-438-9893

Bagels R Bakin
410 Church Ave.
Brooklyn, NY 11218
718-851-1735

M D S Hot Bagels
127 Church Ave.
Brooklyn, NY 11218
718-438-5650

New 13th Avenue Bagel
4807 13th Ave.
Brooklyn, NY 11219
718-633-4009

Bagel Hut
5810 5th Ave.
Brooklyn, NY 11220
718-439-9800

Big Apple Baking Company
215 60th St.
Brooklyn, NY 11220
718-439-3189

Bagels On You
99 Avenue U
Brooklyn, NY 11223
718-630-5271

Dress A Bagel
230 Kings Hwy.
Brooklyn, NY 11223
718-996-3234

Hole In One Bagel
472 Kings Hwy.
Brooklyn, NY 11223
718-627-0273

Metro Bagels
286 Avenue U
Brooklyn, NY 11223
718-449-8906

Jacob's Bagels
750 Flatbush Ave.
Brooklyn, NY 11226
718-284-0400

Bagelicious
7501 13th Ave.
Brooklyn, NY 11228
718-256-0300

Pampered Bagel
7118 13th Ave.
Brooklyn, NY 11228
718-836-6412

Homecrest Bagels
1504 Avenue U
Brooklyn, NY 11229
718-627-0273

Meshuganah Phil's Hot Bagels
1906 Avenue U
Brooklyn, NY 11229
718-743-1515

Bagelicious
1117 McDonald Ave.
Brooklyn, NY 11230
718-377-2952

Kosher Bagel Hole
1431 Coney Island Ave.
Brooklyn, NY 11230
718-377-9700

Arnold's Bagelicious Bagels
23 4th St.
Brooklyn, NY 11231
718-852-0012

Bagels Supreme
203 Columbia St.
Brooklyn, NY 11231
718-243-1030

Bagels Supreme
6220 Avenue U
Brooklyn, NY 11234
718-209-9109

Hot Bagels & More
4710 Avenue N
Brooklyn, NY 11234
718-377-2807

Bionic Bagel
3741 Nostrand Ave.
Brooklyn, NY 11235
718-648-3794

Neptune Bagels
371 Neptune Ave.
Brooklyn, NY 11235
718-646-2210

Bell Bagel & Bialy
8029 Flatlands Ave.
Brooklyn, NY 11236
718-251-9565

Flatlands Bagel Bakery
8101 Flatlands Ave.
Brooklyn, NY 11236
718-251-0903

Hot Bagels
1594 Rockaway Pkwy.
Brooklyn, NY 11236
718-257-3068

Bagel Brothers Bakery & Deli
Main Place Mall
Buffalo, NY 14202
716-856-0159

Bagel Brothers Bakery & Deli
783 Elmwood Ave.
Buffalo, NY 14222
716-882-8885

Bagel Brothers Bakery
Northtown Plaza
Buffalo, NY 14226
716-837-8885

Cookies & Things
211 Glen Cove Rd.
Carle Place, NY 11514
516-742-024

Bagelry
507 Central Ave.
Cedarhurst, NY 11516
516-295-1222

Five Towns Bagels
594 Central Ave.
Cedarhurst, NY 11516
516-569-7070

Bagel Tyme
615 Montauk Hwy.
Center Moriches, NY 11934
516-874-3137

Bagel Bistro
207 Middle Country Rd.
Centereach, NY 11720
516-585-6178

G & D Bagels
2065 Middle Country Rd.
Centereach, NY 11720
516-467-6045

Glazed Goodies
10 E. Buffalo St.
Churchville, NY 14428
716-293-1331

Bruegger's Bagel Bakery
Village Green
Clifton Park, NY 12065
518-383-5814

Bialys Bagels & Butter
Cohoes Commons
Cohoes, NY 12047
518-237-4365

Bagel Chalet
36 Veterans Memorial Hwy.
Commack, NY 11725
516-499-9820

Commack Bagels & Bialys
215 Commack Rd.
Commack, NY 11725
516-499-7606

House Of Bagels
4 Vanderbilt Motor Parkway
Commack, NY 11725
516-499-9677

Bagels of Northeast of Cortland
104 Main St.
Cortland, NY 13045
607-753-6102

DeWitt Bagelry
4451 Genesee St.
De Witt, NY 13214
315-445-0959

Deer Park Bagels
1966 Deer Park Ave.
Deer Park, NY 11729
516-586-9532

Bagelicious Etc.
Main Square Shopping Center
Delmar, NY 12054
518-475-1174

Dix Hills Bagels
697 Old Country Rd.
Dix Hills, NY 11746
516-673-7188

Bialys Bagels & Butter
Columbia Plaza
East Greenbush, NY 12061
518-479-4242

Delicious Cousin's Bagels
117 W. Main St.
East Islip, NY 11730
516-581-1476

Stuff A Bagel
24 E. Main St.
East Islip, NY 11730
516-277-1835

Bagel Patch
2675 N. Jerusalem Rd.
East Meadow, NY 11554
516-499-5939

Bagelicious
1864 Front St.
East Meadow, NY 11554
516-794-0552

Dan's Bagel Cafe
1975 Front St.
East Meadow, NY 11554
516-794-5055

Heavenly Bagels
501 Newbridge Rd.
East Meadow, NY 11554
516-826-7371

Bagel Break
272 Larkfield Rd.
East Northport, NY 11731
516-754-0008

Bagel Master East
1922 Jericho Turnpike
East Northport, NY 11731
516-462-6013

Heavenly Bagels
1006 Oyster Bay Rd.
East Norwich, NY 11732
516-624-9181

Bruegger's Bagel Bakery
Pittsford Plaza
East Rochester, NY 14445
716-248-3110

Bagels Away & To Stay
438 Atlantic Ave.
East Rockaway, NY 11518
516-599-7722

Brians Bunnery
12 Centre Ave.
East Rockaway, NY 11518
516-593-1076

Bagel King
3 Village Shopping Plaza
East Setauket, NY 11733
516-689-7579

Strathmore Bagel
4088 Nesconset Hwy.
East Setauket, NY 11733
516-473-9204

Bagels 'n Brunch
587 Montauk Hwy.
Eastport, NY 11941
516-325-8410

Bruegger's Bagel Bakery
585 Moseley Rd.
Fairport, NY 14450
716-223-3580

Rockaway Bagels
11408 Beach Channel Dr.
Far Rockaway, NY 11694
718-474-1372

G & L Bagels
820 S. Main St.
Farmingdale, NY 11735
516-694-6229

Stuff A Bagel
234 Main St.
Farmingdale, NY 11735
516-420-4287

Bagel Oasis
2318 N. Ocean Ave.
Farmingdale, NY 11738
516-698-3456

Fishkill Hot Bagels
13 Fishkill Plaza
Fishkill, NY 12524
914-897-4594

Orlee Bakery
14414 Northern Blvd.
Flushing, NY 11354
718-358-9421

Paz Bagels
2517 Parsons Blvd.
Flushing, NY 11354
718-463-0316

Bagel Break
4425 Kissena Blvd.
Flushing, NY 11354
718-463-4730

Cross Island Bagels
15369 Cross Island Parkway
Flushing, NY 11357
718-767-0626

T F R J Bagels
3345 Francis Lewis Blvd.
Flushing, NY 11358
718-359-3305

First Class Bagels
25305 Northern Blvd.
Flushing, NY 11362
718-631-0172

Variety Bagels
24936 Horace Harding Expy.
Flushing, NY 11362
718-229-5669

Bagel Oasis
18312 Horace Harding Expy.
Flushing, NY 11365
718-359-9245

Bagels Plus
7039 Parsons Blvd.
Flushing, NY 11365
718-591-3615

Brownies Bagel Bonanza
18524 Horace Harding Expy.
Flushing, NY 11365
718-461-2000

Turnpike Bagels
18502 Union Turnpike
Flushing, NY 11366
718-454-1670

Ain't Just Bagels
9742 63rd Rd.
Flushing, NY 11374
718-459-0204

Me & My Bagel
9301 63rd Dr.
Flushing, NY 11374
718-896-9538

3-Bagel Inc.
9405 63rd Dr.
Flushing, NY 11374
718-997-6444

Austin Street Bagels
6860 Austin St.
Flushing, NY 11375
718-459-1510

Bagel Star
10123 Queens Blvd.
Flushing, NY 11375
718-997-1537

Bagel Stop
10441 Queens Blvd.
Flushing, NY 11375
718-275-4556

E & R Bagel
11210 Queens Blvd.
Flushing, NY 11375
718-263-5858

Glonikos Bagels
4919 30th Ave.
Flushing, NY 11377
718-956-5092

More Than A Bagel
6626 Metropolitan Ave.
Flushing, NY 11379
718-381-0337

A B Bagel Deluxe
6025 Myrtle Ave.
Flushing, NY 11385
718-381-4543

Corner Bagel Factory
6661 Fresh Pond Rd.
Flushing, NY 11385
718-821-0003

A & S Bagel Company
761 Hempstead Turnpike
Franklin Square, NY 11010
516-326-9288

Bagel Go-Round Ltd.
184 New Hyde Park Rd.
Franklin Square, NY 11010
516-488-4110

Bagels Plus
727 Franklin Ave.
Franklin Square, NY 11010
516-872-8475

Magic Bagels of Franklin Square
706 Dogwood Ave.
Franklin Square, NY 11010
516-538-9316

Moshe Bagels
177 W. Merrick Rd.
Freeport, NY 11520
516-379-8481

Bagelman of Garden City
664 Franklin Ave.
Garden City, NY 11530
516-746-2881

Garden City Bagel Shop
313 Nassau Blvd.
Garden City, NY 11530
516-486-4736

Paddy's Glen Oaks Bagel Bakery
25905 Union Turnpike
Glen Oaks, NY 11004
718-343-4801

Goshen Bakery
32 N. Church St.
Goshen, NY 10924
914-294-6233

Bagel Station
99-101 Broadway
Greenlawn, NY 11740
516-261-1837

Hampton Bays Bagel/Deli
52 Montauk Hwy. E.
Hampton Bays, NY 11946
516-728-6759

Hampton Bagels Too
246 Montauk Hwy.
Hampton Bays, NY 11946
516-728-7893

Bagel Emporium of Hartsdale
329 N. Central Ave.
Hartsdale, NY 10530
914-682-0052

Bagel Gallery
534 Smithtown Bypass
Hauppauge, NY 11788
516-360-8406

Sunshine Bagels
383 Nesconset Hwy.
Hauppauge, NY 11788
516-360-0031

Bagel Time
1274 W. Broadway
Hewlett, NY 11557
516-374-6917

Bagelman of Hewlett
1352 Peninsula Blvd.
Hewlett, NY 11557
516-569-8600

Bagel Boss
432 S. Oyster Bay Rd.
Hicksville, NY 11801
516-935-9879

R&R Bagels & Deli
285-14 Broadway
Hicksville, NY 11801
516-935-0510

Best Bagels In Town
480 Patchogue Holbrook Rd.
Holbrook, NY 11741
516-472-4104

Holbrook Bagel Bakery
1073 Main St.
Holbrook, NY 11741
516-981-0848

Hopewell Hot Bagels
532 Rte. 82
Hopewell Junction, NY 12533
914-226-4594

Bagel Tyme
389 Fairview Ave.
Hudson, NY 12534
518-822-1510

Bagel Tyme
41 N. 77th St.
Hudson, NY 12534
518-828-8979

Hunter Mountain Bagels
6 Center Mall
Hunter, NY 12442
518-263-5022

Bagel Bistro
839 New York Ave.
Huntington, NY 11743
516-351-1728

Fabulous Bagels Plus
1058 E. Jericho Turnpike
Huntington, NY 11743
516-673-8480

Super Bagel
24 Wall St.
Huntington, NY 11743
516-423-5798

Glass Oven Bagels
Walt Whitman Shopping Center
Huntington Station, NY 11746
516-421-4404

Gourmet Bagels
107 Walt Whitman Rd.
Huntington Station, NY 11746
516-423-8777

Bagel Patch
84 Carleton Ave.
Islip Terrace, NY 11752
516-581-4949

Bagels On The Terrace
871-8 Connetquot Ave.
Islip Terrace, NY 11752
516-277-4504

Bagels Northeast
Cayuga Mall
Ithaca, NY 14850
607-257-0766

Collegetown Bagels
N. Triphammer Rd.
Ithaca, NY 14850
607-257-2255

Collegetown Bagels
413 College Ave.
Ithaca, NY 14850
607-273-9655

Collegetown Bagels
203 N. Aurora St.
Ithaca, NY 14850
607-273-9835

Bagels On The Bay
16226 Cross Bay Blvd.
Jamaica, NY 11414
718-843-0108

Beach Bagels
8233 153rd Ave.
Jamaica, NY 11414
718-835-7834

Court Bagels
12510 Queens Blvd.
Jamaica, NY 11415
718-793-0882

Uncle Ben's Bagel
8120 Lefferts Blvd.
Jamaica, NY 11415
718-441-3477

Crown Bagel & Chips
10530 101st Ave.
Jamaica, NY 11416
718-805-5860

J & J Bagel
11319 Liberty Ave.
Jamaica, NY 11419
718-738-0407

Bagel Hut
13515 Lefferts Blvd.
Jamaica, NY 11420
718-845-8647

Bagelot
13807 Queens Blvd.
Jamaica, NY 11435
718-739-3939

Flakowitz Bake Shop
433 Jericho Hicksville Rd.
Jericho, NY 11753
516-938-9660

Broadway Bagels
5 Main St.
Kings Park, NY 11754
516-544-0624

Mr. Bagel
730 Ulster Ave.
Kingston, NY 12401
914-338-3080

Smithaven Bagels
119 Alexander Ave.
Lake Grove, NY 11755
516-360-9041

Bruegger's Bagel Bakery
594 New Loudon Rd.
Latham, NY 12110
518-785-4961

Mom's Bagels & Tables
284 Burnside Ave.
Lawrence, NY 11559
516-239-7426

Bagel Street U S A
3611 Hempstead Turnpike
Levittown, NY 11756
516-579-0566

Bagels Best Deli
2999 Hempstead Turnpike
Levittown, NY 11756
516-579-9204

Heavenly Bagels
683 Newbridge Rd.
Levittown, NY 11756
516-931-7218

Stuff-A-Bagel
322 Montauk Hwy.
Lindenhurst, NY 11757
516-225-1916

Wellwood Bagels & Bialys
656 N. Wellwood Ave.
Lindenhurst, NY 11757
516-225-1092

Bagelot Long Island
3113 30th Ave.
Long Island City, NY 11102
718-932-1425

Hoyt Avenue Bagels
2620 Hoyt Ave.
Long Island City, NY 11102
718-956-9730

Crazy Bagel
3241 Steinway
Long Island City, NY 11103
718-267-0928

Mt. Olympus Bagels
3315 30th Ave.
Long Island City, NY 11103
718-721-0600

Eilat Grocery & Bagels
4320 Queens Blvd.
Long Island City, NY 11104
718-784-6222

Holey Bagel
4407 43rd Ave.
Long Island City, NY 11104
718-361-1730

Bagel Boys
3501 Ditmars Blvd.
Long Island City, NY 11105
718-956-1425

Bagel Boys
87 Sunrise Hwy.
Lynbrook, NY 11563
516-599-7078

Malverne Bagels
320 Hempstead
Malverne, NY 11565
516-593-3204

Sir Bagelot Family Restaurant
227 Mamaroneck Ave.
Mamaroneck, NY 10543
914-698-636

Lox, Stocks & Bagels
306 Fayette St.
Manlius, NY 13104
315-682-9065

Best Bagels In Town
632 Broadway
Massapequa, NY 11758
516-795-1055

Buttered Bagel
4917 Merrick Rd.
Massapequa, NY 11758
516-541-4341

Calvert Manor Bagels
1242 Hicksville Rd.
Massapequa, NY 11758
516-799-6528

Stuff A Bagel
177 Jerusalem Ave.
Massapequa, NY 11758
516-797-4089

Triple A Bagels
912 Carmans Rd.
Massapequa, NY 11758
516-541-7415

Leo's Hot Bagels Plus
4882 Sunrise Hwy.
Massapequa Park, NY 11762
516-541-0110

Bagel Lovers
26900 Rte. 112
Medford, NY 11763
516-289-7255

Bold Bagel
3316 Rte. 112
Medford, NY 11763
516-696-3549

Justin's Bagels Ltd.
5507 Nesconset Hwy.
Medford, NY 11763
516-331-3522

Olympic Super Bagel
1699 S. Rte. 112
Medford, NY 11763
516-654-2325

Bagels Unlimited
634 Walt Whitman Rd.
Melville, NY 11747
516-424-7217

Bagel City
1704 Merrick Rd.
Merrick, NY 11566
516-378-3455

Bagel Express Commuter Shop
9 Broadcast Plaza
Merrick, NY 11566
516-868-5327

Bagelman-Deliman
84 Merrick Ave.
Merrick, NY 11566
516-223-7031

Bagel Bill
3 Middle Island Plaza
Middle Island, NY 11953
516-924-7124

Bagelry
115 Mineola Blvd.
Mineola, NY 11501
516-742-3666

Bagels & Buns Cafe
Rte. 17M
Monroe, NY 10950
914-782-5910

Monroe Bagels & Deli
596 Rte. 17M
Monroe, NY 10950
914-783-7831

Bagels-N-More
Corner of Rtes. 59 & 306
Monsey, NY 10952
914-352-0710

Monticello Bagel Corp.
295 Broadway
Monticello, NY 12701
914-794-7746

Bagels Your Way
331 Rte. 25A
Mt. Sinai, NY 11766
516-473-8266

Bagel Bin
308 W. Rte. 59
Nanuet, NY 10954
914-623-1468

Hole in a Roll Bagel
261 Smithtown Blvd.
Nesconset, NY 11767
516-467-0777

David's Bagels
64 N. Main St.
New City, NY 10956
914-639-1664

Lakeville Bagels
2701 Union Turnpike
New Hyde Park, NY 11040
516-347-9192

Bagel Buyer's Directory

New Hyde Park Bagels
930 Hillside Ave.
New Hyde Park, NY 11040
516-354-1330

Bagels & More
40 3rd Ave.
New York, NY 10003
212-674-6817

D & H West Side Bagels
142 E. 16th
New York, NY 10003
212-353-9717

Ess-A-Bagel
359 1st Ave.
New York, NY 10010
212-260-2252

Bagel Buffet
406 6th Ave.
New York, NY 10011
212-477-0448

Chelsea Hot Bagels
300 W. 23rd St.
New York, NY 10011
212-675-7171

Bagels On The Square
7 Carmine St.
New York, NY 10014
212-691-3041

Bagels Around The Clock
637 2nd Ave.
New York, NY 10016
212-725-8755

Daniel's Bagel Corp.
569 3rd Ave.
New York, NY 10016
212-972-9733

3 M Bagel Place
456 3rd Ave.
New York, NY 10016
212-213-3234

Hot Bagels
1372 Broadway
New York, NY 10018
212-768-2867

Bagel Baron of 57th Street
315 W. 57th St.
New York, NY 10019
212-581-9696

Bagel Place
55 W. 56th St.
New York, NY 10019
212-333-3131

Bagelworks
1229 1st Ave.
New York, NY 10021
212-744-6444

Eastside Bagel & Appetizing
1496 1st Ave.
New York, NY 10021
212-794-1403

Pick A Bagel
1083 Lexington Ave.
New York, NY 10021
212-517-6590

Bagel The Bagel
875 3rd Ave.
New York, NY 10022
212-644-5870

Jumbo Bagels & Bialys
1070 2nd Ave.
New York, NY 10022
212-355-6185

Tal Bagels
979 1st Ave.
New York, NY 10022
212-753-9080

B-J Bagels Au Go-Go
130 W. 72nd St.
New York, NY 10023
212-769-3350

Columbia Bagels
2836 Broadway
New York, NY 10025
212-222-3200

Bagel Store & More
1638 York Ave.
New York, NY 10028
212-570-6003

H & H Bagels East
1551 2nd Ave.
New York, NY 10028
212-734-7441

Bagel City
720 W. 181st St.
New York, NY 10033
212-927-3424

Mom's Bagels & Tables
15 W. 45th St.
New York, NY 10036
212-764-1566

Bagelry
1324 Lexington Ave.
New York, NY 10028
212-996-0567

Zabar's Deli & Gourmet Foods
2245 Broadway
New York, NY 10024
212-787-2000

Lox, Stock & Bagel
405-411 Broadway
Newburgh, NY 12550
914-565-0144

Bagel Center
1137 Deer Park Ave.
North Babylon, NY 11703
516-595-9647

Stuff A Bagel
1490 Deer Park Ave.
North Babylon, NY 11703
516-242-9265

Bagel Patch
2474 Jerusalem Ave.
North Bellmore, NY 11710
516-781-4949

Bagels
721 Rte. 25A
Northport, NY 11768
516-754-4121

Strathmore Bagels
1219 Montauk Hwy.
Oakdale, NY 11769
516-567-2515

Bagelry
2941 Long Beach Rd.
Oceanside, NY 11572
516-763-2700

Oceanside
24-hour Bagel Deli
3452 Long Beach Rd.
Oceanside, NY 11572
516-678-6860

Brookville Bagels
Park Plaza Shopping Center
Old Brookville, NY 11545
516-759-5564

Oneonta Bagel Company
171 Main St.
Oneonta, NY 13820
607-433-0162

Bagel Emporium of Ossining
214 S. Highland Ave.
Ossining, NY 10562
914-762-5959

Bridge Street Bagelry & Deli
9 W. Bridge St.
Oswego, NY 13126
315-342-6070

Oyster Bagel
76 South St.
Oyster Bay, NY 11771
516-922-5324

Bagel Basket
350 E. Main
Patchogue, NY 11772
516-758-2902

Bagel Patch
705 Rte. 112
Patchogue, NY 11772
516-289-4949

Bagel Buyer's Directory

Strathmore Bagels
383 E. Sunrise Hwy.
Patchogue, NY 11772
516-654-4277

Daily Bagel
3566 Crompond
Peekskill, NY 10566
914-737-7702

On A Bagel
1861 E. Main
Peekskill, NY 10566
914-736-0001

Town Bagel Shop West
516 Old Country Rd.
Plainview, NY 11803
516-931-5530

Town Bagel Shop
1133 Old Country Rd.
Plainview, NY 11803
516-931-7698

Bagel Emporium of Port Chester
421 Boston Post Rd.
Port Chester, NY 10573
914-937-5252

Bagels Are Us
650 Rte. 112
Port Jefferson, NY 11776
516-474-4208

Bagel Depot
62 Main St.
Port Washington, NY 11050
516-944-8550

Let There Be Bagels
475 Port Washington Blvd.
Port Washington, NY 11050
516-944-8822

The Bagelry
9 Market St.
Potsdam, NY 13676
315-265-9378

Bagel Bin Bakery Cafe
South Hills Mall, Rtes. 9 & 9D
Poughkeepsie, NY 12603
914-297-7474

Hardscrabble Hot Bagels
31 W. Market St.
Rhinebeck, NY 12572
914-876-8025

Bagel Lovers
136 E. Main St.
Riverhead, NY 11901
516-727-5080

Fleischer's Bagels
640 Jefferson Ave.
Rochester, NY 14611
716-235-6080

Bagel Oven
607 Lexington Ave.
Rochester, NY 14613
716-458-6330

Bagel Land
1300 Northgate Plaza
Rochester, NY 14616
716-865-2101

Bagel Land
Irondequoit Plaza
Rochester, NY 14617
716-266-0690

Bagel Bin
1875 Monroe Ave.
Rochester, NY 14618
716-461-4475

Brownstein's Deli & Bakery
1862 Monroe Ave.
Rochester, NY 14618
716-442-2770

Bagel Land
Panorama Outlet Mall
Rochester, NY 14625
716-248-8556

Bagelries
241 Sunrise Hwy.
Rockville Centre, NY 11570
516-766-4422

Bagelries
289 Merrick Rd.
Rockville Centre, NY 11570
516-766-9207

Bagels Your Way II
255 Rte. 25A
Rocky Point, NY 11778
516-744-7949

Bagel Lovers
416 Hawkins Ave.
Ronkonkomo, NY 11779
516-588-7747

Bagels & Bialys
113 Mineola Ave.
Roslyn Heights, NY 11577
516-484-4477

Bruegger's Bagel Bakery
453 Broadway
Saratoga Springs, NY 12866
518-584-4372

Bagels Delox
372 Montauk Hwy.
Sayville, NY 11782
516-563-2716

Scarsdale Bagels
52 Garth Rd.
Scarsdale, NY 10583
914-725-0090

New York City Bagel Co.
1859 State St.
Schenectady, NY 12304
518-370-1800

Bruegger's Bagel Bakery
1634 Union St.
Schenectady, NY 12309
518-393-8667

Manhattan Bagel Shoppe
123 Saratoga Rd.
Scotia, NY 12302
518-399-3877

Bagels Your Way
107 Middle Country Rd.
Selden, NY 11784
516-732-2050

Bagel Mania
863 W. Jericho Turnpike
Smithtown, NY 11787
516-864-2550

Bagel Patch
20 Lawrence Ave.
Smithtown, NY 11787
516-366-4949

Terry Road Hot Bagels
60 Terry Rd.
Smithtown, NY 11787
516-366-3433

Hampton Bagels & Appetizers
819 North Hwy.
Southampton, NY 11968
516-283-9840

Bagels Plus
Rte. 48
Southold, NY 11971
516-765-1162

Bagel Ridge
6 Red Schoolhouse Rd.
Spring Valley, NY 10977
914-425-7714

Bagelry
53 Kendy Dr.
Spring Valley, NY 10977
914-425-2505

Budda's Bagel
55 N. Myrtle Ave.
Spring Valley, NY 10977
914-425-4811

Strathmore Bagels
418 N. Country Rd.
St. James, NY 11780
516-584-8153

Clove Road Bagels
1300 Clove Rd.
Staten Island, NY 10301
718-727-6000

Bagel Buyer's Directory

Stuyvesant Bagels
103 Stuyvesant Pl.
Staten Island, NY 10301
718-816-8010

Bedrock Bagels
1841 Forest Ave.
Staten Island, NY 10303
718-273-1963

R P M Bagels
2162 Forest Ave.
Staten Island, NY 10303
718-876-0140

Bagelicious
1665 Richmond Rd.
Staten Island, NY 10304
718-667-1934

Bay Street Bagel
1130 Bay St.
Staten Island, NY 10305
718-273-0436

Goody's Bagles & Deli
900 Hylan Blvd.
Staten Island, NY 10305
718-273-7164

J & L Bagels
1880 Hylan Blvd.
Staten Island, NY 10305
718-979-1720

B & B Bagels
2175 Hylan Blvd.
Staten Island, NY 10306
718-351-1882

Basically Bagels
99 Guyon Ave.
Staten Island, NY 10306
718-667-8844

Hot Bagels Plus
3211 Richmond Rd.
Staten Island, NY 10306
718-987-6908

Not Just Bagels
655 Rossville Ave.
Staten Island, NY 10309
718-948-2829

M D B Bagels
1180 Forest Ave.
Staten Island, NY 10310
718-720-5827

Puttin On A Bagel Ltd.
714 Castleton Ave.
Staten Island, NY 10310
718-442-8715

Everything On A Bagel
4300 Amboy Rd.
Staten Island, NY 10312
718-984-4300

Hot Bagels Plus Groceries
1307 Arthur Kill Rd.
Staten Island, NY 10312
718-948-3032

Brooklyn Bagel
Staten Island Mall
Staten Island, NY 10314
718-761-7100

Caprice Bakery & Bagels
2813 Richmond Ave.
Staten Island, NY 10314
718-698-4459

Hot Bagels Plus Groceries
3579 Victory Blvd.
Staten Island, NY 10314
718-983-7345

Strathmore's Bagel Factory
2194 Nesconset Hwy.
Stony Brook, NY 11790
516-751-3428

Bagel Boys
214 Rte. 59
Suffern, NY 10901
914-357-9658

Lox, Stocks & Bagels
413 S. Warren St.
Syracuse, NY 13202
315-471-3599

The Bagel Bible

Tappan Bakery
80 Rte. 303
Tappan, NY 10983
914-359-2000

Bagelworks
1026 Broadway
Thornwood, NY 10594
914-769-2080

Bruegger's Bagel Bakery
55 Congress St.
Troy, NY 12180
518-438-3553

Uniondale Bagels
422 Uniondale Ave.
Uniondale, NY 11553
516-483-9800

Magic Bagels
194 W. Merrick Rd.
Valley Stream, NY 11580
516-872-8779

Valley Bagels
155 Rockaway Ave.
Valley Stream, NY 11580
516-825-1647

Bagels And Butts
3240 Railroad Ave.
Wantagh, NY 11793
516-781-8836

Grateful Deli
3047 Merrick Rd.
Wantagh, NY 11793
516-785-3568

Trio Bagel
2845 Jerusalem Ave.
Wantagh, NY 11793
516-781-1001

P S Bagel Company
46 Ronald Reagan Blvd.
Warwick, NY 10990
914-986-9040

Lox, Stocks & Bagels
Salmon Run Mall
Watertown, NY 13601
315-785-6888

U-Need-A Bagels
759 Sunrise Hwy.
West Babylon, NY 11704
516-587-3154

Lox of Bagels & More
89 ½ Main St.
West Glens Falls, NY 12801
518-793-8681

Anchel's Original Bagels
488 Hempstead Ave.
West Hempstead, NY 11552
516-485-6242

Bagel Craft Of West Hempstead
118 Hempstead Turnpike
West Hempstead, NY 11552
516-485-2314

Higbie Bagels
264 Higbie Ln.
West Islip, NY 11795
516-587-1995

Bagel Talk
829 Carman Ave.
Westbury, NY 11590
516-334-2592

Post Bagel
219 Post Ave.
Westbury, NY 11590
516-333-9582

Bagel Brothers Bakery & Deli
5447 Sheridan Dr.
Williamsville, NY 14221
716-632-8885

Bagel Brothers Bakery & Deli
964 Maple Rd.
Williamsville, NY 14221
716-689-8885

Wholey Bagels
797 Yonkers Ave.
Yonkers, NY 10704
914-423-4527

Bagel Mansion
2359 Central Park Ave.
Yonkers, NY 10710
914-779-7008

Highridge Hot Bagels
1805 Central Park Ave.
Yonkers, NY 10710
914-793-2006

Jake's Bagels
Rte. 16
Yorkshire, NY 14173
716-492-4112

NORTH CAROLINA

Bruegger's Bagel Bakery
122 S.W. Maynard Rd.
Cary, NC 27511
919-467-4566

Bruegger's Bagel Bakery
104 W. Franklin St.
Chapel Hill, NC 27516
919-967-5248

Bagel Works Delicatessen
4422 Colwick Rd.
Charlotte, NC 28211
704-364-4000

Bagel Works
6177 E. Independence Blvd.
Charlotte, NC 28212
704-535-0743

Bageltime
1001 E. Harris Blvd.
Charlotte, NC 28213
704-549-8376

Lenny's Little New Yorker Deli
6407 South Blvd.
Charlotte, NC 28217
704-554-6569

Bruegger's Bagel Bakery
626 9th St.
Durham, NC 27705
919-286-7897

Killian's Bagel Bakery
841 Elm St.
Fayetteville, NC 28303
919-323-5084

Bagels
2959 Battleground Ave. #A
Greensboro, NC 27408
919-288-5530

Bagel Cottage
712 Pollock St.
New Bern, NC 28562
919-636-1775

Bagels Plus
1822 S. Glenburnie Rd.
New Bern, NC 28562
919-633-9911

Bruegger's Bagel Bakery
2302 Hillsborough St.
Raleigh, NC 27607
919-832-6118

Bruegger's Bagel Bakery
6274 Glenwood Ave.
Raleigh, NC 27612
919-782-9600

Apple Annie's Bake Shop
Outlet Mall
Wilmington, NC 28403
919-799-9023

Lox, Stock & Bagels
332 S. College Rd.
Wilmington, NC 28403
919-392-0002

OHIO

Lou & Hy's Restaurant & Deli
1949 W. Market St.
Akron, OH 44303
216-836-9159

Hot Bagel Factory
9701 Kenwood Rd.
Blue Ash, OH 45242
513-891-5542

Fresh Bagel Factory
175 E. Alexander Bell Rd.
Centerville, OH 45459
513-434-0020

The Bagel Stop
621 Walnut
Cincinnati, OH 45202
513-723-1903

Skolniks Bagel Bakery
9601 Colerain Ave.
Cincinnati, OH 45251
513-385-5111

Skolniks Bagel Bakery
11700 Princeton Rd.
Cincinnati, OH 45246
513-671-6690

Amster Bagel Bakery
13891 Cedar Rd.
Cleveland, OH 44118
216-321-2102

Better Bagel Company
1903 S. Taylor Rd.
Cleveland, OH 44118
216-321-0738

Bagel Brothers
347 Calhoun
Clifton Heights, OH 45219
513-221-4000

Block's Hot Bagels
6115 McNaughten Center
Columbus, OH 43232
614-863-0470

Block's Hot Bagels
3415 E. Broad St.
Columbus, OH 43213
614-235-2551

Bagel Connection
2705 Far Hills Ave.
Dayton, OH 45419
513-298-3444

Bagel Place
4024 Holland Sylvania Rd.
Maumee, OH 43537
419-885-1000

Bagel & Deli Shop
119 E. High St.
Oxford, OH 45056
513-523-2131

Hot Bagel Factory
7617 Reading
Roslyn, OH 45237
513-821-0103

Hot Bagel Factory
477 East Kemper Rd.
Springdale, OH 45246
513-671-0278

The Bagel Place
4024 Holland
Sylvania, OH 43560
513-885-1000

Barry Bagel's Place
500 Madison Ave.
Toledo, OH 43604
419-241-3354

Barry Bagel's Place
3301 W. Central Ave.
Toledo, OH 43606
419-537-9377

Barry Bagel's Place
492 Southwyck Shopping Center
Toledo, OH 43614
419-866-8984

Kravitz Delicatessen
3135 Belmont Ave.
Youngstown, OH 44505
216-759-7889

OKLAHOMA

Golden Bagels
1009 N. Elm Pl.
Broken Arrow, OK 74012
918-250-9661

The Bagelry
5932 S. Lewis
Tulsa, OK 74105
918-747-2544

The Bagelry
6703 E. 81st St.
Tulsa, OK 74133
918-495-0533

Brooklyn Bagel Company
3535 E. 51st Street
Tulsa, OK 74133
918-747-1475

OREGON

Bagel Man
1461 Siskiyou Blvd.
Ashland, OR 97520
503-488-0357

New York Bagel Boys
11667 S.W. Beaverton Hillsdale
Beaverton, OR 97005
503-641-3552

Bagel Stop
661 N.E. Greenwood Ave.
Bend, OR 97701
503-389-3363

Bagels From the Heart
325 N.E. Kearney Ave.
Bend, OR 97701
503-389-5434

Val's Homemade Bagels
11525 S.E. Hwy. 212
Clackamas, OR 97015
503-656-2777

Bagel Bakery
795 W. 8th Ave.
Eugene, OR 97402
503-342-4390

Humble Bagel Company
2435 Hilyard St.
Eugene, OR 97405
503-484-4497

Portland Bagel Bakery & Deli
222 S.W. 4th Ave.
Portland, OR 97204
503-242-2435

Kornblatt Delicatessen & Bagel
628 N.W. 23rd Ave.
Portland, OR 97210
503-242-0055

Bagel Land
4118 N.E. Fremont St.
Portland, OR 97212
503-249-2848

New York Bagel Boys
4775 S.W. 77th Ave.
Portland, OR 97225
503-292-6667

PENNSYLVANIA

Atsa Bagel
1636 Union Blvd.
Allentown, PA 18103
215-820-5355

Home of the Ultimate Bagel
1542 E. Pleasant Valley Blvd.
Altoona, PA 16602
814-942-2435

A&S Bagels
5613 Bensalem Blvd.
Bensalem, PA 19020
215-638-1665

Bagel Builders
305 Neshaminy Mall
Bensalem, PA 19020
215-322-5767

Breakfast Club
19 E. State St.
Doylestown, PA 18901
215-348-1108

Skolniks Restaurant & Bakery
Palmer Park Mall
Easton, PA 18042
215-252-8007

Bagel Basket
3 E. 18th St.
Erie, PA 16501
814-456-1080

Bagel House
317 Main Ave.
Hawley, PA 18428
717-226-9443

Bagel House
110 7th St.
Honesdale, PA 18431
717-253-3566

Bagel Train
Stourbridge Mall
Honesdale, PA 18431
717-253-0913

Basically Bagels
3rd Ave.
Kingston, PA 18704
717-288-6000

That's Entertainment
197D Greenfield Rd.
Lancaster, PA 17601
717-295-1770

Bagel Place
60 Pocono Blvd.
Mt. Pocono, PA 18344
717-839-9301

Skolniks
2 Penn Center Plaza
Philadelphia, PA 19102
215-563-8299

Bagel Builders
The Gallery Mall, No. 1
Philadelphia, PA 19107
215-238-0760

Nate's Hot Bagels
1619 Grant Ave.
Philadelphia, PA 19115
215-676-3772

Brooklyn Bagels
813 Hendrix
Philadelphia, PA 19116
215-464-2330

Vaughn's Bakery
908 Bethlehem Pike
Philadelphia, PA 19118
215-233-1055

Brooklyn Bagels
905 N. 3rd St.
Philadelphia, PA 19123
215-627-5288

Roxy Bagels
499-A Domino Ln.
Philadelphia, PA 19128
215-487-1727

Lane Bakery
1922 E. Washington Ln.
Philadelphia, PA 19138
215-548-4080

Bella Bagel
2233 S. Woodstock St.
Philadelphia, PA 19145
215-467-4005

Philadelphia Bagel Company
1100 S. Delaware Ave.
Philadelphia, PA 19147
215-336-7211

South Philly Bagel Factory
2655 Sheridan
Philadelphia, PA 19148
215-334-0492

Brooklyn Bagels
7412 Bustleton Ave.
Philadelphia, PA 19152
215-342-1661

Bustleton Bagelry
8338 Bustleton Ave.
Philadelphia, PA 19152
215-725-5512

Bageland
2120 Murray Ave.
Pittsburgh, PA 15217
412-521-1067

Bagel Hut
325 Mount Lebanon Blvd.
Pittsburgh, PA 15234
412-343-2245

Cibrone & Sons Bakery
1231 Grove Rd.
Pittsburgh, PA 15234
412-885-6200

Bagel Express
115 Oakland Ave.
Pittsburgh, PA 15213
412-683-9644

Bagel Wich
Keyser Oak Shopping Center
Scranton, PA 18508
717-347-5877

Pocono Bagels Shawnee
Shawnee Square
Shawnee Del., PA 18356
717-476-8805

Bageland
3022 Banksville Rd.
South Hills, PA 15216
412-531-1067

Pocono Bagels
Olympia 611 Plaza
Stroudsburg, PA 18360
717-424-2073

Skolniks Restaurant & Bakery
Lehigh Valley Mall
Whitehall, PA 18052
215-266-7141

RHODE ISLAND

Bagels Etc.
259 Country Rd.
Barrington, RI 02806
401-247-1213

Rainbow Bakery
800 Reservoir Ave.
Cranston, RI 02910
401-944-8180

Barney's
727 East Ave.
Pawtucket, RI 02860
401-727-1010

Bagels East
63 Dorrance Plaza
Providence, RI 02903
401-454-1793

Bagels East
135 Elmgrove Ave.
Providence, RI 02906
401-331-6195

Bagels East
961 Namquid Dr.
Warwick, RI 02888
401-737-0269

Bagel's 'N More
105 Franklin St.
Westerly, RI 02891
401-596-9954

SOUTH CAROLINA

Ashley South Windermere Bakery
65 Windermere Blvd.
Charleston, SC 29407
803-763-4125

Nathan's Deli
1836 Ashley River Rd.
Charleston, SC 29407
803-556-3354

Cribb's Bakery
1030 Harden St.
Columbia, SC 29205
803-799-5034

TENNESSEE

Gottliebs Deli
5062 Park Ave.
Memphis, TN 38117
901-763-3663

Nashville Bagel Company
3009 West End Ave.
Nashville, TN 37203
615-329-9599

TEXAS

Bagel's Hot Jumbo
307 W. 5th St.
Austin, TX 78701
512-477-1137

Bagelsteins Delicatessen
8104 Spring Valley Rd.
Dallas, TX 75240
214-234-3787

New York Deli
3301 Oaklawn
Dallas, TX 75219
214-522-3354

The Bagel Emporium
7522 Campbell Rd.
Dallas, TX 75248
214-248-1569

Bagel Chain
5555 W. Lovers Ln.
Dallas, TX 75209
214-350-2245

Reichman Strictly Kosher Deli
7517 Campbell Rd.
Dallas, TX 75219
214-248-3773

Grace's Restaurant & Deli
315 E. Franklin Ave.
El Paso, TX 79901
915-533-2910

New York Bagels
9724 Hillcroft
Houston, TX 77096
713-723-5879

The Hot Bagel Shop
2009 S. Shepherd
Houston, TX 77019
713-520-0340

Alfred's of Houston
9123 Stella Link Rd.
Houston, TX 77025
713-667-6541

Gelfand's Deli
10001 Westheimer
Houston, TX 77042
713-780-0443

Gugenheims Deli
1708 Post Oak Blvd.
Houston, TX 77056
713-622-2773

Bagel House & Deli
13323 Nacogdoches Rd.
San Antonio, TX 78217
512-653-2122

O & H Rare Foods
111 N. 25th St.
Waco, TX 76710
817-753-5291

UTAH

Wildflower Bakery
4387 Harrison Blvd.
Ogden, UT 84403
801-521-6040

Brackman Brothers Bagel Bakery
859 E. 900 S
Salt Lake City, UT 84105
801-322-4350

Brackman Brothers Bagel Bakery
1520 S. 1500 E
Salt Lake City, UT 84105
801-466-8669

VERMONT

Bennington Bagel Co.
241 Main St.
Bennington, VT 05201
802-447-3308

Bagel Bakery
139 St. Paul St.
Burlington, VT 05401
802-658-0563

Bruegger's Bagels
81 Church Street
Burlington, VT 05401
802-860-1995

G T Bagel Factory
35 White St.
Burlington, VT 05403
802-863-3644

G T Bagel Factory
29 College Pkwy.
Colchester, VT 05446
802-655-2660

Vermont Bagel Works
Rtes. 11 & 30
Manchester Center, VT 05255
802-362-5082

Burlington Bagel Bakery
89 Main St.
Montpelier, VT 05602
802-223-0533

Bagel Bakery
992 Shelburne Rd.
South Burlington, VT 05403
802-864-0236

Better Bagel
Taft Corners Shopping Center
Williston, VT 05495
802-879-2808

VIRGINIA

Chesapeake Bagel Bakery
3610 King St.
Alexandria, VA 22302
703-379-6462

Chesapeake Bagel Bakery
601 King St.
Alexandria, VA 22314
703-684-3777

Bodo's Bagel Bakery Sandwich
1418 Emmet St. N
Charlottesville, VA 22901
804-977-9598

Holey Roll Bagels Etc.
3813 S. George Mason Dr.
Falls Church, VA 22041
703-998-8083

Chesapeake Bagel Bakery
6138 Arlington Blvd. #A
Falls Church, VA 22044
703-534-3533

Mr. J's Bagels/Deli
1635 E. Market St.
Harrisonburg, VA 22801
703-564-0416

Not Just Bagels
859 J. Clyde Morris Blvd. #J
Newport News, VA 23601
804-599-3556

New York Bagel Shops
161 Granby St.
Norfolk, VA 23510
804-627-2345

Bagel's Bakery
10831 W. Broad Street Rd.
Richmond, VA 23233
804-346-8785

Bagel Place
9049-1 W. Broad St.
Richmond, VA 23294
804-273-0600

Chesapeake Bagel Bakery
8420 Old Keene Mill Rd.
Springfield, VA 22152
703-451-4788

Bagelworks
3972 Holland Rd.
Virginia Beach, VA 23452
804-498-7785

Chesapeake Bagel Bakery
2217 Old Bridge Rd.
Woodbridge, VA 22192
703-497-0300

WASHINGTON

New York Bagel Boys
Crossroads Shopping Center
Bellevue, WA 98007
206-641-5300

New York Bagel Boys
2222 220th SE
Bothell, WA 98021
206-485-5300

Original Brooklyn Bagel
15159 N.E. 24th St.
Redmond, WA 98052
206-562-2435

Seattle Bagel Bakery
1302 Western Ave.
Seattle, WA 98101
206-624-2187

Bagel Stop
408 E. Broadway
Seattle, WA 98102
206-325-9407

Spot Bagel Bakery
1815 N. 45th St.
Seattle, WA 98103
206-633-7768

Bagel-Deli Company
1309 N.E. 43rd St.
Seattle, WA 98105
206-634-3770

New York Bagel Boys
4764 University Pl. NE
Seattle, WA 98105
206-523-1340

Bagel-Deli Company
340 15th E
Seattle, WA 98112
206-322-2471

Bagel Oasis
2112 N.E. 65th
Seattle, WA 98115
206-526-0525

WISCONSIN

Bagel Mill
523 W. College Ave.
Appleton, WI 54911
414-739-9090

Lox, Stock & Bagel
1300 S. Webster Ave.
Green Bay, WI 54301
414-432-9244

Sueann's Bagels
1933 Main St.
Green Bay, WI 54302
414-469-7727

Sueann's Bagels
2216 S. Ridge Rd.
Green Bay, WI 54304
414-494-7777

Bagels Forever
2947 University Ave.
Madison, WI 53705
608-231-2427

Bakery And The Bagel
7475 Mineral Point Rd.
Madison, WI 53717
608-833-0770

Bagel Deli
383 W. Brown Deer Rd.
Milwaukee, WI 53217
414-228-8060

Kramers Kosher Corner
5101 W. Keefe Ave.
Milwaukee, WI 53216
414-442-2625

Bagel Boys Bakery & Deli
3247 W. Vliet St.
Milwaukee, WI 53208
414-344-8060

Miller Bakery
1415 N. 5th St.
Milwaukee, WI 53212
414-347-2300

CANADA

The Bagel Factory
12411 Horseshoe
Richmond
British Columbia
604-272-1798

The Bagel Bar
1218 Bute
Vancouver
British Columbia
604-684-5882

Bageland
1689 Johnson
Vancouver
British Columbia
604-685-1618

Bageland
1610 Robson
Vancouver
British Columbia
604-684-8575

Bageland
810 Quayside NW
Vancouver
British Columbia
604-520-1124

Bageland
333 Brooksbank
Vancouver
British Columbia
604-983-2572

The Bagel Bar & Deli
2 Bloom E
Toronto
Ontario
416-922-5800

Bagel Beat
3452 Danforth Ave.
Toronto
Ontario
416-699-9528

Bagel Haven Bakery Ltd.
800 Steeles W
Toronto
Ontario
416-738-5673

Bagel Hut
1000 Eglinton W
Toronto
Ontario
416-781-9181

Bagel Paradise
953 Eglinton W
Toronto
Ontario
416-787-8670

Bagel Plus Ltd.
634 Sheppard Ave. W
Toronto
Ontario
416-635-9988

The Bagel Stop
Fairview Mall
Toronto
Ontario
416-498-6261

The Bagel Restaurant
285 College
Toronto
Ontario
416-923-0171

Bagel & Wok
4544 Dufferin
Toronto
Ontario
416-665-2218

Bagel World Coffee Shop
336 Wilson Ave.
Toronto
Ontario
416-635-5931

Bagelicious
7355 Bayview
Toronto
Ontario
416-731-3363

Bagel Makers
5150 Yonge
Toronto
Ontario
416-395-0450

Bagels Galore
First Canadian Place
Toronto
Ontario
416-363-4233

Bagelrye Ltd.
7 Grantbrook
Toronto
Ontario
416-222-6308

Bagel Etc.
4320 St. Lawrence
Montreal
Quebec
514-845-9462

Bagel Factory
74 Fairmont W
Montreal
Quebec
514-272-0667

The Bagel Place
1616 St. Catherine
Montreal
Quebec
514-931-2827

The Bagel Place
1455 Peel
Montreal
Quebec
514-848-1802

Bagel Shop Inc.
263 St. Viateur W
Montreal
Quebec
514-276-8044

Bagelettes Inc.
6135 de Maisonneuve
Montreal
Quebec
514-276-2972

Authors' Note

Is there a favorite bagel shop you'd like to see listed?
Let us know. Write to:

My Favorite Bagel Shop
c/o The Globe Pequot Press
P.O. Box 833
Old Saybrook, CT 06475